WOKE*d* UP!

FINALLY PUTTING AN AX TO THE TAPROOT OF WHITE SUPREMACY AND RACISM IN AMERICA

KEVIN McGARY

RATIONAL FREE PRESS

Toronto · San Jose · Boise

WOKEd UP! *Finally Putting An Ax to Taproot of White Supremacy and racism in America*

Contact the author at: KevinMcGary@RationalFreePress.com

Published in Canada and the United States by Rational Free Press

Other titles by this author:

The War on Women From The Root To The Fruit!

JUST "Justly Justice"

Instanity!

ISBN 978-1-7772018-4-5

For speaking/engagements, please contact:

Jackie Jones, Truth PR

Jackie@TruthPR.com

(662) 259-0988

WOKE'd Up!

Finally Putting An Ax To The Taproot Of
White Supremacy and Racism In America

BY KEVIN McGARY

TABLE OF CONTENTS

DEDICATION

I dedicate the entirety of this book and any positive insights or "good" that results from it to my Father!

Father, this is your work; you graciously bestowed on me wisdom and insight in these matters, so breathe afresh on it that it may produce "good fruit in due season."

I also dedicate this to all the people who have been diligent in praying and asking God for answers to combat the negative trajectory of woke culture to heal our land. This book confirms your prayers have been heard, and this book is one response to your diligence!

Lastly, this book is dedicated to the "rising" generation. The rising generation has been maligned and abused by nefarious ideologies and agendas seeking to destroy their soul. I pray this book provides renewed hope and freedom that comes from being "set free." Since truth is the single most crucial factor to being "set free," here you go..........

ADVANCE PRAISE

Kevin McGary is a gifted researcher and writer with masterful skills in dissecting and framing current socio/cultural issues. He is my resource for Critical Race Theory (CRT) issues, "fatherhood" and unity & reconciliation! Kevin's keen foresight puts him at the forefront to effectively battle major problems plaguing America. With this book, readers will surely gain knowledge and strategy to combat one of the most significant cultural battles of our time…"WOKEism!" I encourage you to read and support McGary and his admirable works.

-- Dr. Jim Garlow, CEO, Well Versed

Kevin McGary's book "WOKEd UP" is a masterpiece. With insights that cut straight to the heart of pressing issues facing America, he peels back the deceptive facade of wokeism and exposes the "super power" of truth needed to win the perpetual battle of good versus evil. Kevin is articulate, brilliant and courageous in championing the Godly values that so urgently need to be passed on to our children. You will be better equipped to confront the weaponized narratives of Darwinism, Racism and White Supremacy being used to divide the country. I believe the Lord has raised up Kevin McGary for such a time as this! You will be challenged, inspired, and empowered to win over the culture after reading McGary's book WOKEd UP!

--William J. Federer, nationally known speaker, best-selling author, and president of Amerisearch, Inc.,

PREFACE

You will find *WOKEd Up!* is a timely read because it addresses the most pressing issues facing America and all global societies (past and present). On your journey through *WOKEd Up!,* you will discover the root cause of institutionalized racism, "White Supremacy," sexism/misogyny, genocide, Marxism, and eugenics. You'll see these topics investigated from a perspective you may not have heard or considered before, but most assuredly, the root cause of each of these social maladies will be fully exposed.

Over the past decade, global societies have experienced an acceleration (and seeming urgency) surrounding issues of "race." All societies are inundated with accusations and reprisals about "racism." Surely, racism has always existed, but now racism has been given its special designation that encompasses all people and all societies (past, present, and future). For many, the desire to observe the world and all actions and interactions through the prism of race has turned the social domain of "race" into a veritable religion. With the zeal and respect, it garners, "race worship" is certainly akin to worshipping at an altar of a religious idol (or doctrine). Utilizing racialized ideology, people are "guilted," shamed, and denounced to the extent that they are even "canceled." Today, the open-minded way of simply observing race and its potential limitations and liabilities is challenged by a very different approach that relies almost entirely upon race as the primary construct used to categorize and define all relationships and interactions.

Observing the world strictly through the "lens" of race is considered "reality" for many. However, because race issues are pervasive and the consequences potentially severe, it is long past time we pursue a healthy and proper perspective on the issue of "race" and the related issue of "White Supremacy."

If we are sincere about having the right perspective on racism and White Supremacy, we need to discover and understand with whom, how, and why it started. With that knowledge, we finally begin to do something meaningful to correct the racist ideas and move toward human harmony. Unfortunately, it's easy to remain complacent and dismiss the need to intentionally look into race issues by saying it began with the "fall of man" in the Garden of Eden. "It's just an evil like all other evils we must now live with," Some people say. While this is true, it's not the whole story.

Before accepting cultural narratives (and resulting dictates) about race totally and uncritically, isn't it necessary and prudent to determine for yourself the foundations to confirm their actual relevance for how you perceive yourself and others? In other words, if there were evidence that our current paradigms about "race" and White Supremacy are built on gross misconceptions due to false narratives and perpetuated by people's malevolent intentions, wouldn't you like to know and more fully understand?

Instead of accepting racism as merely an evil that exists due to "fallible" humanity, let's consider whether 19th, 20th, and 21st-century racism and White Supremacy are institutions stemming largely from the works and ideas of one individual? Can we identify the works and ideas and find an actual starting point for their origins and transmission to the world?

Suppose there is a way to isolate specific times and events that prove racism and White Supremacy actually became a firestorm because of one person. Would you like to know who that individual is? If there is a way to debunk prevailing narratives asserting racism as being unbridled

4

and "systemic" (everywhere), and "White Supremacy" as being wholly built-in to all "White" people based upon their skin color, would you like to know?

Here's the big question everyone should ask themselves: "If there is a way to see the entire paradigm of "race" from its "root," would you assuredly take a (metaphorical) 'ax' to it to destroy its corrosive impact and effects permanently?"

This book uncovers and exposes racism and White Supremacy at their respective roots to allow readers to take a veritable "ax" to "chop them down." This journey of discovery will not target just any old "root"; it will isolate and permanently uproot the behemoth culturally-accepted constructs of race and White Supremacy by exposing the "taproot." Taproots can be basically defined as the primary root systems and central elements that allow for the growth or development of an entity. To finally put an end to destructive narratives and corrosive actions of racism and White Supremacy, we will aim to "ax" the taproot after it has been fully exposed.

Get ready: *WOKEd Up!* delivers more exhaustive explanations for some of our most pressing issues, then empowers readers to "chop down" the exposed taproot of racism and White Supremacy. In the end, it will be incumbent upon you (the reader) to get WOKEd Up and definitively "put an ax" to racism and supremacy. At the end of every chapter, I use emojis to characterize emotions I went through while researching and writing this book; you will see my emotions ranged between

Melancholy   *Anger*   *Mind-blowing*

Are you ready to awaken? Let's get WOKEd Up!

INTRODUCTION

It does not take a majority to prevail... but rather an irate, tireless minority, keen on setting brushfires of freedom in the minds of men.

~ Samuel Adams

Humankind has always been in a perpetual and eternal fight for "good vs. evil." This fight began in the garden of Eden and has intensified and raged over millennia. Too often, the intensity and momentum of the battle between these two forces, coupled with our emotional investment in one side or the other, blind us to what should be obvious. The obvious fact is: Mankind is fallible and therefore prone to making huge errors. Unfortunately, our errors most often go in one direction, the direction of evil instead of good.

We might want to give humankind the benefit of the doubt, but our fallible nature is consistently attracted to and bent toward evil. In the fight of good vs. evil, we face an epic battle similar to David *vs.* Goliath, as reported in the Old Testament, 1 Samuel 17. Goliath, a giant, represents evil; David, a humble shepherd, represents good. As we're swept and gripped into the epic battle, we face the "giant" of culture as it causes shifts, drifts and rifts in society. In this book, we face an old giant who has made its mark and now must be confronted by a brave "David."

The "Davids" of today are those who will not bow to the whims of "culture" that seek to divide and instill guilt and shame. Modern Davids must remain principled and steadfast in defiance while readying to confront this giant. Though they clearly don't have the boastful swagger, might, and strength that Goliath showed, today's Davids are fearless and steadfast in determination to combat the giant (culture) and win! A David is not propelled by reckless and boastful hubris. He is not motivated by personal self- confidence; David's confidence is squarely in the power and might of the "God of Abraham." With God's assurance, David turns back Goliath's boasts with the truth. He ultimately defeats the giant by his bold stand and actions!

The David and Goliath story – the faithful shepherd *vs.* the boastful giant-- is most *apropos* to the current cultural confrontation. Culture and society seem like omnipotent (all-powerful) forces making demands destined to progressively and perpetually transform culture and society, while a seemingly small and insignificant *remnant* is positioning to combat these insidious cultural perturbations negatively impacting current and future generations. [1]

David fought Goliath by taking a determined stand against him. It looked like he was "out-manned" (his adolescence and stature seemed no match for a full-grown man and giant). He had no formal training in battlefield tactics nor experience in warfare. Most importantly, he was seemingly "outgunned": Facing a giant foe with full armor, shield and spear, David showed with a sling and just a few smooth rocks. So, what was David's secret weapon? David stood on God's Word and "truth." He did prevail with his few stones alone, but his determined zeal rested upon God's prompting.

The same zeal and determination that David possessed and prevailed with is energizing the remnant with today. Like David, we are being propelled to take a determined stand, armed with the truth, against the giant of diabolical elements within culture.

When culture rants, rages, and feigns utter emotionalism about whatever the "outrage" of the moment seems to be, the response should be the truth's calming, confident voice. The truth alone represents the weapon of determination and the rock that will prevail in bringing down the giant. Irrespective of the torrent of emotional whims that seek to undermine, transform and utterly destroy foundations of civil societies, the truth is the ultimate weapon that will prevail in turning back the tide.

So-called popular culture has been shifting to the point that the most pervasive existential threat to the foundations of civil societies is now the cultural embrace of "wokeism." This insidious threat manifests itself in many ways. Wokeism injects itself into every domain as it seeks to undermine and redefine the family structure, embraces and encourages violent popular culture, enshrines subpar public schools and educational standards, asserts gratuitous secularism, and excuses almost any form of negative personal behaviors (even various psychoses). Woke individuals claim these domains need permanent structural redefinition due to their protracted history of hegemonic patriarchy leading to "structural racism."

Suppose "wokeism" is a euphemism for being awakened to some newfound enlightened truth. In that case, it's incumbent upon everyone to determine and confirm the real truth. Getting to the nub of real truth allows the capacity to declare whether indeed you're part of the woke masses or are a resister against the movement.

Truth has "super-power" One of my favorite Bible verses is John 8:32, which reads, "You will know the truth, and the truth will set you free." Notably, the truth provided David with the determination and faith in his sling and rocks that enabled him to slay Goliath, the taunting giant. The truth has been proven ever since as fundamental for setting people free.

A great example in American history is the life of the honorable Frederick Douglass. In his autobiographies, Frederick Douglass confirmed that upon overhearing his enslavers discussing how reading and education has the capacity to set slaves "free," he resolved to become masterful in reading and public speaking. God's divine providence, coupled with Douglass' mastery in reading and oratory, set and kept him free! Truth always prevails, so we need to embrace it.

This book aims to finally illuminate and confront the truth about racism and White Supremacy. Even if truth challenges prevailing narratives and is wholly inconvenient, this book specifically intends to combat all misinformation, revisionist histories and flat- out lies that impact our engagement in culture and society. Only by intentionally confronting the "giant" of our time ("cultural wokeism"), will we finally be able either align further with it, or be set free from it.

Assumptions and prevailing narratives that encourage many to virtue signal and socially preen about being woke may not carry the same significance after this reading. All schemes to undermine our soul and defraud us of a happy and truly successful future for our family/progeny, community and nation will be exposed here. That said, there is a distinct possibility that wokeism may become unpopular after reading this book. Since it is not written merely to encourage or discourage wokeism (that's just the focal point for revealing the truth), the ultimate outcome is personal and solely up to you. Either way, the truth will be exposed.

One of America's Founding Fathers, Samuel Adams, reminds us that even as a seeming "majority" (including global mass groups, individuals, industry etc.), enshrines unfettered chaos and tumult by reliance on grotesque ideologies, those who tirelessly commit to encouraging non-ideological free-thinking, will ultimately prevail! This gives hope and anticipation of seeing a "free" America again! Please consider this wise forethought: *It does not take a majority to prevail... but rather an irate, tireless minority, keen on setting brushfires of freedom in the minds of men ~ Samuel Adams*

It's way past time to discover and unleash truth... So let's get WOKEd Up!

CHAPTER ONE
AWAKENED TO WOKED

"Have we reached the ultimate stage of absurdity where some people are held responsible for things that happened before they were born, while other people are not held responsible for what they themselves are doing today?"

~ Thomas Sowell

Get WOKEd UP!

There is so much more to wokeism than meets the eye. The term woke often occurs in conversation, yet few seem to understand it. We tend to drift into the culture of wokeism because it feels *emotionally* right. *Wokeism's principles, however, are* ill- defined. The definition of woke is purposely nebulous, amorphic, and ever-changing.

Wokeism's lack of principled definitions is why the fact-based material within this book is so significant. It's time for wokeism and its fundamental roots to be fully illuminated and exposed. Once you know the facts, the changes in your mindset should be life-altering.

A woke person can be summarily defined as someone who is "hip," well-informed, and fully cognizant of social injustices. The term woke refers to someone who is consciously intentional about remaining vigilant to "injustices." These days, wokeism primarily focuses on a person's relative sensitivity to prejudices and racial and social injustices. As practiced, today's woke movement demands we interact with one another with full consciousness of "class," race, and gender differences in mind; no more "casual" opportunistic connections. The more sensitive someone is, ranging up to being a raging activist hysterically spouting racialized ideology, the more woke the person is deemed. Dissenting voices to wokeism are summarily deemed as racist.

Simply assessing someone's level of being woke (or wokeism generally) is not the same as hurling insults. However, accusing a person of not being woke can be weaponized to become insulting. These days, the weaponization of wokeism has produced gratuitous charges of racism, White supremacy, White privilege, and myriad false narratives about the need to guilt, condemn, shame, and utterly disparage all White people and their progeny. Weaponized wokeism can be quite cruel.

While it is difficult to define accurately, there are many scholars who have written about wokeism. For example, in a recent column in American Greatness, Victor Davis Hanson, Scholar and Distinguished Fellow at Stanford's Hoover Institution, characterized the era of woke this way: *"Wokeism's natural logic is to destroy the lives of people of both genders, of all races, and—if need be—of those of every age, all to leverage an otherwise unworkable ideological agenda."*

He further states, *"wokeism has been described by its critics as the omnipresent use of race—and to a lesser extent, gender—to replace meritocracy and thus ensure equality of result. What follows from implementing that ideology are reparatory actions to reward those of the present by atoning for the injustices done to others in the past."*

Hanson continued, *"it (wokeism) is nihilist and destroys everything it touches. It is a cruel thing to indoctrinate children with the lie that they are innately guilty of oppression due to their skin color. One accurate definition of racism is collective ill-treatment of an individual due to his innate appearance—on the pretext that such bias is deserved, given the target is deemed mentally, spiritually, or morally inferior because of said traits…. In sum, wokeness is not about kindness, equality, fairness, or morality."*

As a final note, Hanson asserts, *"We know wokeism is both contrary to human nature and antithetical to democracy and constitutional government….Without public support, it has instead embraced an entire array of cruel, Soviet, and Maoist means to achieve its own self-interested ends….No wonder the woke, so-called 'humanists' are the first to resort to Trotskyization and iconoclasm. They are masters of censoring, blacklisting, scapegoating, deplatforming, ritual humiliation, doxxing, cancel-culture, ostracism, and disbarring."* [2]

Victor Davis Hanson perfectly summarized the definition, dangers, and ultimate outcome of wokeism. At this point in time, it has evolved into an insulting, corrosive and dangerous cliché. Words have power, and tactically, woke (or wokeism) is used as a cudgel to demand and force compliance to the ever-evolving ideologically "progressive" culture.

An Awakening?

One would think the fundamental point of being woke is to be awakened. We should all want to be enlightened and awakened to what *is really* happening. For example, if systemic racism is really occurring and is everywhere, as posited by "wokesters," we should want to be awakened to do something about it. On the other hand, if wokeism unprincipledly relies on false narratives and is born of nefarious forces intended to manipulate cultures and societies, then we should want to be awakened to those (albeit) inconvenient truths as well.

Logically, we must be ready to confront the truth wherever we find it. If it challenges us to reject our prevailing thoughts and opinions, so be it. If it goes against our socio/political ideology, so be it. If by way of facts and truth, we are presented with wholly incongruent and inconvenient roots of wokeism that force us to change direction away from personal "leanings" and preferences, thereby adopting of a new mindset, so be it! Die-hard Progressive woksters generally tend to be driven by emotions; there is no doubt that newfound truths will be held with some level of internal turmoil, suspicion, and rejection. But the plethora and preponderance of truth will prevail.

Personal honesty is key. To sincerely explore this subject matter requires people willing to be thoughtful and honest with themselves. Deception, especially self-deception, will not produce anything fruitful; it only encourages more momentum toward further lies and deception, which erodes and ultimately destroys the soul. Consider these questions about your sincere mindset:

- Should I attempt to understand wokeism better?

- Am I willing to consider points of view that may differ from my predisposition?

- Am I willing to explore facts and truths even if they are "inconvenient" to my prevailing thoughts?

- If new facts are presented that empower me to understand factual root causes of

- White Supremacy and racism in America, am I willing and able to embrace a change in mindset?

- Am I going to allow myself to be "WOKEd UP?"

Preeminent American economist and historian Thomas Sowell, illuminates the level of absurdity that must be confronted in an attempt to overcome arcane ideological mindsets. Sowell poses a question that must be pondered as it confirms and reveals our current stage of absurdity: *"Have we reached the ultimate stage of absurdity where some people are held responsible for things that happened before they were born, while other people are not held responsible for what they themselves are doing today?" ~ Thomas Sowell*

Let's get WOKEd Up!

CHAPTER TWO
"WHO LET THE DOGS OUT?"
THE PROCESS OF UNLEASHING "RACISM" AND "WHITE SUPREMACY"

"With so many things coming back in style, I can't wait until morals, respect and intelligence become a trend again"

~ *Denzel Washington*

Back in the day, "Who Let the Dogs Out" was a very popular song ("Baha Men," 2010).[3] Even today, this song plays at various venues. For me, this song carries personal and culturally poignant meanings.

On the personal side, "who let the dogs" out reminds me of a time when I owned an Akita dog. Her name was Sparkle. She was an incredible specimen and a stunningly beautiful "beast." The reason why I call her a beast is, while she was wonderful and loving to any humans she met, she was a literal killer for all other dogs she came in contact with. She had to be leashed or she would harm any other dogs in the vicinity. One day she was unleashed, jumped over my backyard fence, and went hunting for any other dogs. Unfortunately, she found a neighbor's dog running free and she pounced, killing the dog instantly.

When an awesome force is unleashed, it can have terrible and profound consequences; the resulting carnage can sometimes be incalculable. I have no doubt, that every one of my neighbors who saw and heard the brief encounter my dog had with the other dog, still lives with unforgettable horror about the encounter that day...Including myself! "Who let the dogs out" still rings in my ears, but not for its catchy tune and hip melody. It rings because it brings back memories of my dog Sparkle, my beautiful beast wreaking havoc when she was unleashed.

Racism and White Supremacy are awesome sinister forces that have long been unleashed. They are not figments of the imagination; they have proven to possess extraordinary powers that kill, steal, and destroy. Millions of people have been killed, trillions of dollars have been stolen from economies and entire civilizations have been squandered and destroyed due to unleashing of racism and White Supremacy.

How did we arrive at a historical point whereby ancient evils like racism and supremacy can be brought forth and unleashed? Is there such a thing as unleashing evils that preexisted? Certainly! When new distinctions are brought forth, previously unknown or unthinkable possibilities can be instantly created. This can generate context and possibilities for actions that accelerate and instantiate social/cultural changes. In essence: "words matter!"

Words Matter

New possibilities of thoughts and actions are created via linguistic distinctions (created words). Remember, God framed our world by just speaking it into existence. Similarly, we can frame new concepts, ideas, actions, and perspectives through our words. This is not trivial; human beings use linguistic distinctions to create, change and differentiate the world with new possibilities for action. This awesome human capacity has led to tremendous innovations and positive change. But there have also been some distinctions that were created and, when unleashed, brought forth a world bearing significant negative changes.

Metaphorically reflecting on the situation with my dog, when something is leashed, it is tethered, held back, and restrained, and from that point can be controlled. Conversely, the act of unleashing unlocks and removes constraints allowing what was previously leashed to freely roam uncontrolled. This applies to all domains. It is true for our physical world (i.e., my dog being unleashed), our thoughts (unleashing the mind to embrace unlimited "free-thinking" and new possibilities) and language. Language empowers people to make new distinctions that then provide a world of new possibilities and actions.

When new distinctions and nomenclature are created, new possibilities and horizons of thought are unleashed. Most times, this means new innovations and institutions are formed, and societies are propelled forward. But what happens if there are negative distinctions brought forth? Just as newly created words/nomenclature/distinctions bring positive discourse and outcomes, they can also generate negative ones. The biggest factor in the positive or negative impacts on social change depends on the source.

Based on the source, new words can be neutral (for instance, a hip cliché that goes viral) whereby nothing changes except new words are gradually added to our dictionaries. Anybody can (and does) create new words. But rarely do new words go "viral." If however, distinctions are created by leaders who are recognized as having "authority" with proven competencies, their newly created words carry significance. There are implications for words coming from leaders or experts, so recklessly unleashing newly-created vocabulary can lead to terrible long-lasting consequences. Therefore, all newly-created distinctions should be carefully considered, and especially if the distinction has profound world-changing implications.

"Woke," "Wokeism," even "WOKEd UP!" are good examples of benign distinctions that virally proliferated. As they catch traction in culture and are virally adopted, they're perhaps viewed as indicative of "bad grammar" and mere hip new cliches. In and of themselves, however, these distinctions present no obvious or profound consequence. But, when coupled with narratives about racism and White Supremacy, they can take on meanings potentially producing tremendous global change. There have already been some changes produced by woke nomenclature. Some of the social changes resulting from the nomenclature of woke involve: (1) actions taken to "guilt" others; (2) forcing the embrace of automatic distrust and division based on immutable characteristics (like color of skin or "whiteness"); and (3) outright condemnation of others just because of dissenting opinions and for possessing lesser ideological zeal. Unfortunately, many people are quite willing to point fingers and castigate others as a way to virtue-signal and socially preen about their full embrace of "woke," while tacitly deeming all others as racists. These are some of the negative ways words can be used to influence culture and change societies.

The best way to throttle new distinctions as they are unleashed and virally spread throughout the culture is to define them accurately. Words that carry nebulous or amorphic meanings can be dangerous. They can be twisted to apply almost anywhere and used as a cudgel against those who simply live by dissenting ideology or morals.

As words are used to frame our world, the words generate underlying *themes*. For instance, when the term "race" was codified, it allowed the opportunity to study the various ethnicities to determine if there were indeed race distinctives. Instead of the world being appreciated from the standpoint of humanity as a single reflection of humanity (generally), race became a distinction used to "classify" individual humans and groups based on preference/partiality and dichotomies of inferiority and superiority. Race was an invented linguistic distinction, but it has become the genesis of some of the most historically negative outcomes that we still are trying to work through to this very day.

"Race" unleashed

The term "race" was unleashed without proper definition. It provides a great example of what can happen when a word is invented without considering impacts and outcomes. DNA studies confirm there are marginal differences between those of White ethnicities and those with higher melanin counts (Blacks and others with darker skin). Race therefore hardly qualifies as a worthy distinction.

Practically speaking, this makes race hard to define. Perhaps it is still undefined. Is race strictly understood based on skin color? Is it synonymous with, and should be considered, as interchangeable with the term "ethnicity?" What is the distinction between race and ethnicity? Without proper context and distinction, race has taken on a life unto itself; it has been recklessly unleashed and ultimately weaponized as the primary way to assert supremacy.[4]

"Race" was unleashed as a new distinction in 1700's. Johann Friedrich Blumenbach, a German naturalist and anthropologist (1752–1840), was the first to divide the human species into five races in 1779. In 1793, his research led him to create classifications based on intricate studies of skulls and brain formations. From his studies, Blumenbach classified the Caucasian race (Europe, the Caucasus, Asia Minor, North Africa, and West Asia), the Mongolian race (East Asia, Central Asia and South Asia), the Aethiopian race (Sub-Saharan Africa), the American race (North America and South America), the Malayan race (Southeast

20

Asia). As his works propagated over the following decades, additional races and classifications would continue to be added.[5]

Blumenbach's work is significant to us today because he found *no* scientific reason or rationale to classify Blacks as inferior to other races, and he rejected all such notions. Notwithstanding Blumenbach's findings, naturalists in his era embraced what is deemed "scientific racism," which classifies and distinguishes races as inferior to Whites (Whites/Caucasians being the "superior" race); they used Blumenbach's works as justification for race classification and discrimination. Blumenbach may be the "father of race classifications," but he did not embrace racism. People after him would attempt to weaponize race by asserting superiority, harboring their own malicious, malevolent, racist intent. Their intentions can by no means be based on scientific principles.

Race weaponized

After race classification was unleashed and accepted by the scientific community, it was unscrupulously weaponized to justify partiality and favoritism between people groups. Most notably, race was malevolently enlisted to help assuage any guilt while giving credence to evil people hell-bent on maltreatment of people groups summarily deemed "sub-human." Some of the most notorious maltreatments can be best discerned by reflecting on the treatment of imported enslaved Africans to America as compared to others. Due to the immutable characteristic of skin color alone, African slaves had been deemed members of the "Black race" and subjugated to another newly enshrined race category of "Whites" (Caucasians). Notably, with race classifications there was an entire demographic of American Whites that (without guilt or remorse) felt Blacks were sub-human and should be viewed and treated as "property." Because of constantly emerging "scientific evidence" (albeit skewed and flawed), Whites viewed themselves as being the most favored race. Therefore, all other races were summarily viewed as lower, only partially evolved, or even sub-human. *Where did the slave-owning Whites get the idea that Blacks were a race that was not fully human and therefore could/should be treated in inhumane ways?*

Though the scourge of slavery raged in the Southern States in America prior to and into the mid 1800's, subjugating people groups based solely on race claimed full "scientific" justification in the mid-1800's. New studies and theories about race were championed and relied upon as confirmation of racial differences. Unfortunately, these theories not only cemented the resolve of racists to continue guiltless maltreatment of members of the Black race via slavery (also prolonging it), they also confirmed and enshrined standards of "White supremacy" solely based on the newly created linguistic distinction of "race."

Who could have been so cold and calculating to the extent of encouraging further unleashing and proliferation of racial distinctions? Who ultimately provided confirmation and justification for grotesque racist partiality and maltreatment of Blacks under the auspices of "White supremacy?"

Here's a hint: It came from an elitist who was viewed as having scientific and anthropological authority; his work notoriously incorporated new linguistic distinctions as part of his "theory." To this very day, he has mass appeal globally. Who was he? The culprit who rejected Blumenbach's findings that Blacks were not to be sub-categorized, and malevolently asserted otherwise, was none other than Charles Robert Darwin!

A rudimentary understanding of the power of linguistics and the part it can play in the unleashing of new actions, ideas, and philosophies helps grasp how one man can bring forth generations of suffering and destruction even through wholly unproven "theories." Darwin unleashed a beast that carried new anthropological, sociological and ontological significance. Among numerous other insidious notions, his ideas institutionalized racism and White Supremacy, allowing it to become part of the interwoven fabric of all societies and cultures worldwide.

WOKEd Up! is designed to unpack and present unfiltered truth so we can be set free! In truth, the complex of language/words/distinctions/social vocabulary is used to help us distinguish the world. Some words help create entire nomenclature and thoughts that then can rapidly translate into new levels of thinking and innovation. For this reason, words should be scrutinized and precisely defined because once unleashed, as we've seen, they can produce myriad unintended consequences. If someone who is heralded as an authority creates and unleashes new distinctions, then new social patterns and accepted parlance can be quickly disseminated, allowing the world to change practically overnight.

Through Darwin, racism and White Supremacy were fully linguistically distinguished, given authoritative credence, and institutionally accepted. The transition from language to idea system meant Blacks suffered by being labeled "sub-human" (and treated as such), and it prolonged the incalculable suffering of Blacks continuing to this very day! This is how racism and "White Supremacy" were unleashed, and our world is forever changed...*for the worse!*

While Charles Darwin is a notable "scientific icon," this doesn't preclude him or his diabolical theories from serious scrutiny. Actor Denzel Washington provides humor and wisdom to help govern our

23

assessment of Charles Darwin and his machinations: *"With so many things coming back in style, I can't wait until morals, respect and intelligence become a trend again" ~ Denzel Washington*

Are you "Woked Up!" yet?

CHAPTER THREE

WORSHIPPING AT THE ALTAR OF "DARWIN"

"Violence as a way of achieving racial justice is both impractical and immoral. Violence is impractical because it is a descending spiral ending in destruction for all. It is immoral because it seeks to humiliate the opponent rather than win his understanding: it seeks to annihilate rather than convert. Violence is immoral because it thrives on hatred rather than love."

~**Reverend Dr. Martin Luther King Jr.**

Since releasing his works, encompassing new theories about life, its origin, and classification, Darwin has been worshiped!

Charles Darwin and his works are revered in scientific and anthropological communities and worldwide societies and cultures. His theories dominate the base curriculum in all educational institutions from kindergarten through college. Further, his works have impacted cultural norms, government policies, and the progression (or barbaric regression) of societies since their advent in the 1800s.

The worship of Darwin is near-universal. But why? Is Darwin a person deserving great praise? Is the extolling of "Darwinism" (proliferation of his theories and works) warranted?

Consider: If it can be confirmed that Darwin unleashed racism, would he be deserving of universal praise, or disdain? If it can be proved he unleashed White Supremacy, would he deserve worship, or rejection? If we find he gave cover for misogyny/sexism, would he still deserve unwavering support? What if he helped unleash genocide and eugenics, and as a result, over 100 million innocent lives were lost?

Honestly speaking, if Darwin is found to be the root cause for unleashing even one of the social plagues, it would be bad enough, warranting a thorough rejection of his legacy going forward. At the very least, Darwin's legacy would need to reflect his diabolical deeds with at least a strong footnote.

In that same way, what if we find he was singularly responsible for unleashing and institutionalizing *all of these* (racism, White supremacy, misogyny/sexism, genocide and eugenics)? Sound hyperbolic? Let's see!

It would defeat the purpose of this book to veer into purely ideological paths and push conspiratorial assertions that fault someone without factual justification and confirmation. We must soberly realize that since the fall of man in the garden of Eden, evil was unleashed, and as a result, there have been unscrupulously notorious people driven by manifest evil. Human evil has persisted and opportunistically spread as far as its many participants would take it. The participants extended evil when they participated in extreme partiality (racism & supremacy), encouraged unequal and malicious treatment of women/females, and possessed fervent xenophobia, which led to the extermination of tribes and ethnicities outside of their own. Genocide and eugenics fall into that category of evil.

All these human atrocities existed in some form and were carried out in eras predating Darwin. So, how can anyone then assert Darwin is singularly responsible and should be held with contempt due to the profound impact of the worst horrors and atrocities in human history? The answer, as discussed above, is *language*. Darwin and his followers recklessly unleased newly-generated linguistic distinctions that gave these kinds of evil a justification, momentum, and acceleration.

The rest of this book documents how Darwin's theories and assertions gave rise to the worst atrocities in human history. Notably, Darwin's works did not blare out through a megaphone to demand people accept his ideas. Instead, the ideas in his writings were subtle and seductive. Without fanfare, Darwin made assessments and announced theories, which merely declared how he felt the world is constituted; he didn't have to scream or shout demands for the embrace of his new distinctions (and the resulting changes in societal parlance). He just provided "scientific" and anthropological assessments that were seductively compelling as they unfortunately catered perfectly to evil hearts of fallen humankind. Compared to wholesome truths, it seems that when unleashed, evil more easily catches traction and momentum amongst the masses.

Darwin's Subtly Diabolical Seductions

To this very day, great numbers of everyday people believe and embrace Darwin's theories. Because Darwin was perceived as a scientific and anthropological authority (in some circles, regarded as a genius), many believe Darwin's theories irrespective of their diabolical precepts. Darwin's specific (albeit inconvenient) assertions (posited as theories) that unleashed America's racism and White Supremacy surely demand our full attention.

Even though Darwin shares the exact same birthday as Abraham Lincoln (February 12, 1809), the two men were destined to lead the world in opposite directions. Borrowing from the Declaration of Independence, Lincoln reasserted "all men are created equal" in his November 19, 1863,

Gettysburg address. Around the same time, Darwin's theory of evolution was unleashed, and it declared that men were not created at all. Instead, they evolved. Additionally, Darwin proclaimed that all men are not equal, as he held that some are more evolved than others. Note how diametrically opposed the two worldviews are.

The original title of Darwin's first book and most famous work illuminates his heart and intentions. It also confirms how he redoubled racism and White supremacy in America. Darwin's signature work was titled "On the Origin of Species by Means of Natural Selection, or *The Preservation of Most Favored Races in the Struggle for Life* (1859)." The book's title alone confirms Darwin made a distinction between races. In this and subsequent writings, he was fervent in assuring supremacy existed. Darwin asserted the Caucasian race ("White" Europeans) as a superior race and likened Blacks to apes and savages. Darwin went out of his way to characterize an idyllic and almost angelic caricature for Whites, while gratuitously putting Black and Aborigines at the bottom of the evolutionary scale (just slightly above parasitical levels). His writings asserted empirical evidence that there are distinctions between races, with Whites (Caucasians) as "supreme," and all races locked in perpetual competition in *"the struggle for life."* If you're awakening, this should begin to clarify the "scientific" instantiation of White Supremacy.

Remember: New distinctions are created in language, and language gives rise to meaning and vocabulary. Using his authority as an anthropologically inclined scientific mind, Darwin created new linguistic "realities" that men are not equal and should be treated differently. This is "classic" racism. He asserted that Caucasians are genetically superior to all other races; this gave rise to diabolical mindsets determined to live out and exert superiority over all others.

As confirmation and justification for his racist distinctions, Darwin cited and wholly relied on leading ethnologists of the day who evaluated the size of the cranial cavity with racial and ethnic hierarchies. Here is an example of some of his cranial studies: *The belief that there exists in man some close relationship between the size of the brain and the development of the intellectual faculties is supported by the comparison of skulls of savage and civilized races of ancient and modern people, and by the analogy of the whole vertebrate series. Dr. J. Barnard Davishas proved by many careful measurements, that the mean internal capacity of the skull in Europeans is 92.3 cubic inches; in Americans87.5; in Asians 87.1; and in Australians only 81.9 cubic inches.*[6]

Again, Darwin asserted a direct correlation between cranial size and intellectual capacity and proceeded to rank racial and ethnic hierarchies (always resulting in "White" Europeans at the top of the hierarchical scale). White supremacy was defined and enshrined by Darwin's work. To accept Darwin's theories and fundamental arguments is to accept and embrace racism.

The following is what historian, John Koster, has noted about Darwin's view on race: "[Darwin] *never considered "the less civilized races" to be authentically human. For all his decent hatred of slavery, his writings reek with all kinds of contempt for "primitive" people. Racism was culturally conditioned into educated Victorians by such "scientific" parlor tricks as Morton's measuring of brainpans with BB shot to prove that Africans and Indians had small brains, and hence, had deficient minds and intellects. Meeting the simple Indians of Tierra del Fuego, Darwin wrote: "I could not have believed how wide was the difference between savage and civilized man; it is greater than between a wild and domesticated animal . . . Viewing such a man, one can hardly make oneself believe that they are fellow creatures and inhabitants of the same world."*[7]

Darwin was a true believer in his theories. He consistently justified racist ideas and precepts to facilitate reasons for disparate treatment between races. Author Richard Weikart has extensively studied and published on Darwin's views' content, origins, and effects.[8] Weikart explains Darwin's racism as follows:

Four elements of Darwinian theory provided fuel for exterminationist racism. First, Darwin propagated Malthus's idea that the population has a tendency to expand faster than the food supply, a point that seemed confirmed by the rapidly expanding European population. Second, Darwinian evolution required variation within species, and most Darwinists in the nineteenth century considered human races either subspecies or even separate species. Ernst Haeckel, the most famous Darwinist in late nineteenth-century Germany, for example, divided humans into twelve species and even grouped these species into four separate genera! Third, because of the population imbalance, individuals within a species have to compete for scarce resources in a struggle for existence. Many Darwinists, including Darwin and Haeckel, argued that this competition-to- the-death occurred not only between individuals, but also between groups, such as tribes or races. Finally, many Darwinists argued that Darwinism undermined traditional Judeo-Christian ethics, including its stress on the sanctity of human life. Blended together with their new conception of the value of human life and the competitive struggle between organisms, racial extermination seemed (at least to some) natural and inevitable — indeed, even beneficial and progressive.[9]

Weikart's observations about Darwin and other influential biologists like Haeckel confirm their undeniably racist assertions. The determined act of disregarding the fact that all men are created "equal," then attempting to categorize and confirm distance and distinction between races, constitutes racism.

Racism Defined

The sub-title of Darwin's original works (referring to "most favored races"), actively asserting Caucasian (White) supremacy, degrading Blacks as equivalent to apes and savages, and justifying maltreatment due to subhuman categorizations, confirms how racism was unleashed and instantiated by Darwin. His unleashing of reprobate theories asserting supremacy and human degradation meant that there was a new, modern, "scientific" justification for treating men differently for the first time in human history. The effects were horribly disproportional.

The point is, that Darwin's status as a preeminent naturalist biologist and scientific "mind" allowed him to unleash newly developed linguistic distinctions that undermined humanity. It undermined Blacks more than any others, as Blacks were conveniently classified as apes and savages. Before Darwin's proclamations that formed anthropological vernacular undergirding racist theories, racism and White Supremacy lacked the stamp of objective truth, and thus they were mostly opportunistically experienced out of evil hearts of those hell-bent (literally) on racism.

"Scientific Justification" For White Supremacy

The 1700s and 1800s enshrined slavery in North and South America, so indeed, people adopted socially and culturally dominant attitudes. That said, Darwin was the first of his stature to provide "scientific justification" for partiality-based, inhumane and disproportionate treatment based on anthropological studies. That justification led to ontological institutionalization of racism and White Supremacy. From that point forward, racism was recognized, encouraged, and upheld. Think about it: Racism can be summarily defined as the overlaying of collective (institutionalized) maltreatment of individuals based solely on immutable characteristics (in this case, color of skin); every marked individual is connected to entire people groups that are then deemed as undeserving of equal treatment because of their "inferiority" (identified by color of skin). This ideology is exactly what Darwin widely disseminated and unleashed. "Biological arguments for racism may have been common before 1859, but they have increased by orders of magnitude following the acceptance of evolutionary theory…" ~Stephen Jay Gould, Harvard University. [10]

Under the influence of Darwin's theories, White Supremacy accelerated as the Caucasians were enshrined as superior to other races. All other races were deemed a variation of a sub-classification or even sub-human. Because Darwin distinguished these classifications, we can see Darwin's works unleased the racist, enslaving, and genocidal worldview.

Darwin's works have been celebrated. His theories are still (mostly) trumpeted as scientific fact. The worlds' elites still bow at his altar. Entire governments eagerly imbibe his theories and use his works to justify evil policies and schemes for more power and control over their citizens or subjects. Thinkers who challenge Darwinism face losses of jobs and exclusion. It's as if there were an insatiable need and desire to inculcate evil. Since its original publishing, Darwin's works (in some form) have justified inflicting horrific human suffering on innocents for some of the worst and most notorious mass- murdering regimes in history. Despite the acceleration of horrific evils, most people continue to revere Darwin as great and virtuous man. For some reason, Darwin has been insulated from scrutiny, never blamed for institutionalizing racism and White Supremacy. *That all changes – starting now.*

When they even think about Darwin's history of ideas, many will brazenly attempt to cover for his racist evil ideas and results. It's ironic and unbelievable that while certain "wokeness" advocates wax hysterically about White Supremacy and racism in America (past and present), they also eagerly and grotesquely defend Darwin. Why? Are Darwin enthusiasts simply insincere and unprincipled? Unless they take a stand against his theories and machinations, we cannot take the wokesters seriously or view them any other way.

People exercising "woke hysterics" and projecting guilt onto others about the atrocities of slavery should be reminded about how Darwin-style ideas impacted the infamous Supreme Court's decision in the Dred Scott case. Dred Scott's outcome came as a direct result of ideas that Darwin tried to "prove" true using his theories. The Dred Scott case considered whether all humans have the right to freedom and found that no person of African ancestry could claim citizenship in the United States. The decision stated: *"Slaves had...been regarded as beings of an inferior order...so far inferior, that they had no rights which the white man was bound to respect; and that the Negro might justly and lawfully be reduced to slavery for his benefit."*[11] (*Scott v. Sandford*, 60 U.S. (19 How.) 393, 407-(1857).

When will "wokesters," college professors, and institutions of learning (K-12 and universities) take a definitive stand against inconvenient truths and facts about Darwin? Fortunately, the preponderance of evidence and facts have pushed some to begin to awaken truly. One university has seen enough evidence and is committed to not continually defending the indefensible; they have already called out Darwin as a racist:

According to a University of Sheffield (England) teaching and research handbook, theory of evolution mastermind Charles Darwin "held racist views" because his science was used to "justify white male superiority."[12]

Closing the loop: The point of becoming woke is to be fully enlightened and awakened fundamentally. When you are awakened to the fact that Darwin is principally responsible for amplifying White Supremacy, myriad bigotry, and racism in America, you can't go back to "sleep."

Get WOKEd Up!

Carefully reading the factual background of Darwin and his works, some obvious yet gnawing issues arise. Some questions that deserve an answer are:

- **Why would someone of Darwin's stature summarily reject Blumenbach's scientific findings (no distinction between races) and continue headlong with his theories asserting there is some level of equivalency between Blacks and apes? And, asserting White Supremacy over all other races/ethnicities?**

- *Using today's "cancel culture" standards, why hasn't Darwin been canceled in all schools, with all his theories expunged from the curriculum? (Unbelievably, Darwin's covert racist white supremacist views still permeate the K-college curriculum!)*

- *Why isn't Darwin rejected and denounced as the reigning promulgator of ontological and anthropological distinctions used to support racism and White Supremacy in America?*

- *Given the historical facts about Darwin's "scientific" teachings underlying racism and White Supremacy, shouldn't individuals, institutions, school systems or education boards denounce him? Suppose they still fully embrace his works while refusing to renounce and denounce Darwin. Wouldn't they themselves (by today's definition) actually be deemed racist and White Supremacists?*

- *Look inward and ask yourself: Given Darwin's racist and supremacist ideas clothed as "science," can you say Darwin was evil? If so, should you be teaching (K-college) students evil?*

- *Realizing Darwin pressed racist and White Supremacist ideas as unquestionable science, shouldn't people who still worship and extol him be themselves deemed racist and White Supremacist? (You can't have it both ways!)*

The Reverend Doctor Martin Luther King Jr. provides a poignant context for how we should begin to perceive and assimilate our thoughts about using violence as a tool for justice. Darwin's "justification" for White Supremacy and racism necessarily evokes and promotes violence. However, violence precipitated by Darwinist theories seems to be somehow "excused…Until now! *Please hearken to Dr. Kings words of wisdom: "Violence as a way of achieving racial justice is both impractical and immoral. Violence is impractical because it is a descending spiral ending in destruction for all. It is immoral because it seeks to humiliate the opponent rather than win his understanding: it seeks to annihilate rather than convert. Violence is immoral because it thrives on hatred rather than love." ~* **Rev. Dr. Martin Luther King Jr.**

35

Let's get seriously WOKEd Up!

Chapter Four
Unleashing "religion" of "wellborn" onto the unborn

"A nation that kills its children in the womb has lost its soul"

~ Mother Theresa

Through a more intentional look into the roots of Darwin's theories, we can better discern the power of words and distinctions, illuminate the roots of racism and White Supremacy, and deeply expose Darwin's darkened soul and associated motives. Since the truth (alone) sets us free, we should begin feeling the initial process of being "set free" from many previously-held false narratives. Admittedly, anyone can be seduced and compelled to hold false narratives about Darwin and his associated works. His theories can be seductive, especially if there are motivations and desires to assert "class" or racial superiority. We should ask ourselves, "With science already confirming otherwise, what could have possibly motivated Darwin to defiantly assert and demand White supremacy?" A study of some of Darwin's family roots provides clear confirmation.

As mentioned, Johann Fredrich Blumenbach (1752-1840) provided Darwin with a great foundation giving insight and perspective on the classification of human races. Following in Blumenbach's footsteps, Darwin became an esteemed Naturalist, Anthropologist, and Scientist. Regrettably, similarity in scientific focus is about all Darwin and Blumenbach had in common. Darwin rejected much of Blumenbach's findings and charted a diabolical path that would negatively impact the course of human understanding and development for generations.

One of Darwin's earliest and most significant influencers was his close family member Thomas Malthus (1766-1834). Malthus was an 18th-century British philosopher and economist; he was also Darwin's first cousin. Malthus philosophies had a tremendous influence on Darwin's scientific theories. Most notably, Malthusian theories led Darwin to reject Blumenbach's scientific findings confirming Blacks had no cognitive or intellectual deficiencies (as compared to Whites). Instead, Darwin chose to conclude and "scientifically" assert otherwise.

Thomas Malthus authored extreme philosophies that not only encouraged some level of paranoia but also (as with Darwin) encouraged scientific assertions of "superiority." Malthus argued that there would never be enough food to keep up with the demands of natural (organic) growth in human populations. He concluded that humans would always suffer from famine and misery because it would consistently outpace the food supply. Malthus philosophies were infused with dramatic paranoia about impending famine, war, and or disease; he saw these threats prompt the anticipated need to protect superior (more evolved; elitist) ethnicities. Malthus inferred a growing need to protect increasingly scarce resources from rising ethnic populations (especially those reproducing in large numbers). These philosophies impacted Darwin's theories in profound ways.

Malthus' philosophical works encouraged Darwin to consider the implications of overpopulation and how it was necessary to have variability in different populations. Undoubtedly, Darwin used Malthus ideas as the impetus for his theories of natural selection.

Darwin came to believe that (left to their own natural course) populations would breed beyond their means, encouraging competition in the effort to exist. Darwin observed populations would produce some individuals that were stronger and better equipped to survive, and those individuals would produce more and eventually dominate. This reasoning was the primary assertion in his evolutionary and natural selection theories. This reasoning was also the motivation for the rejection of Blumenbach.

It can be surmised that Darwin rejected Johann Blumenbach's assertions that Blacks are equal to Whites because he perceived an impending threat of what he believed was a scarcity of resources. Characterizing some ethnicities as sub-human, and making clear distinctions that assert a superior classification of the White race, is necessary if there is paranoia about the scarcity of resources. Darwin's firm embrace of Malthus' paranoid philosophies about "scarcity of resources" likely prompted Darwin to characterize Blacks as subhuman. Ultimately, Darwin's theories not only culminated in assertions of White Supremacy and racism but also helped usher in a sinister tactic designed to help "scientifically justify" the elimination of "undesirables" (all other ethnicities). With help and collaboration from another family member, Darwin would put one of his most evil racist machinations, posing historical ramifications, into action.

Notably, Darwin's had another (younger) first cousin, Francis Galton. Galton greatly admired his older cousin's works and became one of his most fervent disciples. At the time, Darwin was heralded, and his works were viewed as enlightened and profound. Darwin's works and associated theories profoundly affected his younger cousin, Galton, who was in Birmingham, England, in 1822 and as a scientist and anthropologist pioneered work in human intelligence. In his various fields of studies, Galton was particularly enamored by the idea of classifying humans through the use of origins and classifications. Those concepts were front and center in cousin Darwin's work. Serious scientific study led to the synthesis of ideas, which propelled Galton to become one of the preeminent minds that brought about the field of statistics. Galton became known for applying statistics to challenge prevailing concepts and conventional thinking. This ultimately led him to classify and grade humans. Galton's initial works involved scoring people by looks (beauty); he became obsessed with the idea of classifying humans based on heredity and assessing how talents and flaws are passed on through the generations[13]

Like his older cousin Charles Darwin, Francis Galton was so obsessed with the commitment *to the preservation of the most favored races* that the families of Darwin and the Galtons intermarried. Darwin so stridently believed in White supremacy and preserving what he thought were "superior" genes, in his paranoia, he married his first cousin and had ten children with her. Actually, Darwin was following in the footsteps of his older cousin Thomas Malthus. Many years earlier, Malthus was also married to a first cousin. His sordid example, coupled with paranoia about the scarcity of resources and the urgent need to maintain what was believed to lead to the purity of White supremacy, no doubt motivated Darwin to do the same.

Based on Darwin's theories, the close family members undoubtedly felt intermarrying would allow them to preserve their pure genetic disposition and produce progeny with above-average intellect and talent. In his book on the history of twins, Galton wrote:

If [five percent] of the cost and pains were spent in measures for the improvement of the human race that is spent on the improvement of the breed of horses and cattle, what a galaxy of genius [we could] create! We might introduce prophets and high priests of civilization in to the world, as surely as we can propagate idiots by mating cretins. Men and women of the present day are, to those we might hope to bring into existence, what the pariah dogs of the streets of an Eastern town are to our own highly- bred varieties.[14]

Among the many people stricken by Darwinist elitism, there is a notable disdain for people they summarily classify as "common" men. Anyone not deemed to be in the elitist class or categories is automatically disparaged using sometimes shockingly hateful terms. To further cement Galton's characterizations of those he deemed as "idiots" and "cretins" (those in non-elite categories), his scientific and anthropological studies picked up momentum. In 1883, Galton coined the word "eugenics." Eugenics would be used to "scientifically" base his study of human evolution.

Naming and Claiming Eugenics

Galton's new term, eugenics, derives from Greek words and means "well-born." Again, taking cousin Darwin's works to heart, Galton asserted that human anthropology consisted of Aryan supremacy (White Supremacy) and is undergirded by "survival of the fittest." Classifications, statistics, and his (mostly predetermined) anthropological assessments unleashed Galton's new terminology to a hungry and racist elitist class looking for full justification to continue maltreatment of all other ethnicities. Instead of leaving it to men's free and voluntary interactions to prosper humanity, Galton didn't want to leave it to "chance" that men could "naturally evolve." He was motivated to try to manipulate humanity by encouraging the genetic evolution of society for the good of the species. Galton's approach is fundamentally eugenics! Galton's desires and intentions were to undermine development and wholly disparage those of any non-Aryan race; he used newly developed rudimentary classifications and categories to quantify disparate treatment amongst races.

In his hubris, Galton felt so strongly about eugenics that he anticipated others would accept and fervently embrace it; like a "religion." "In an unpublished science fiction novel, *The Eugenic College of Kantsaywhere* (1910), Galton imagined a society forcibly governed by eugenics, in which every child takes an exam, and only the fittest are allowed to reproduce, while those who score lowest are shipped off to distant colonies. At his most enthusiastic, Galton imagined eugenics becoming a "new religion," a "creed,", the "religion of the future." Invisibly to many, Galton's dreams have come true! Eugenics has been embraced like a religion. Due to Darwin's racist-rooted ideas and Galton's diabolical embracing of them, eugenics (in one form or another) still dominates all cultures and societies on the planet.

Darwin's work and theories profoundly affected his cousin. Darwin's and Galton's theories together can be deemed the "father of Eugenics." The impacts of their ideas, now recognized as unscientific, nevertheless continue to reverberate through culture. Most regrettably, their works are used as justifications to classify, marginalize and dehumanize all races outside of pure White/Aryan while extolling the White Supremacists and elite.

Meanwhile, the gospel of eugenics spread worldwide and proved particularly popular in the United States in the 1920s and 1930s and in Nazi Germany. The term "eugenics" lost its luster when the Nazis murdered anyone deemed mentally, physically or racially defective. "Eugenics" became a taboo subject after it was loaded with white supremacy and fascism connotations. And it's true that Galton also categorized the races into a hierarchy, as when in an 1873 letter to the Times he argued Africa should be given to the "industrious, order-loving Chinese."[15] Galton genuinely saw himself as a humanitarian. Eugenics would do efficiently and humanely what nature would otherwise do cruelly. The choice was either: (1) let the unfit and unwanted be born and live miserable lives of illness and failure; or (2) make sure such humans were never born in the first place. Which is kinder?

Doctors today still recommend parents let severely disabled babies die out of mercy, and over 90% of fetuses with Down Syndrome are aborted. We carry out the eugenics agenda today more than we may like to admit. When looking at the false narratives (and associated linguistics) from the cousin's Darwin and Galton, it is impossible to ignore the facts confirming eugenics' insidious background and history. It is based on the notion of "well-born." That, in and of itself, is "supremacist!" The notion of "well-born" was codified in racism and instantiated to uphold "White Supremacy." These noxious ideas all intertwine with Darwinian theory and Galton's new "eugenics" agenda.

The world greedily imbibed Galton's eugenics potion. Hateful racists, White Supremacists, slaveholders, and especially people in political authority inclined toward tyranny followed Darwin and Galton's playbook to the letter. In their day, they were "following the science!" They then had "full justification" to unduly punish any with differing God-given immutable characteristics (like skin color or non-Aryan ethnicity).

Eugenics and Its Impact on Societies

Since Darwin's theories rejected the notion of God (as creator, designer, and sustainer of the universe and of humankind), maltreatment of others came easy to Darwin followers. Little notice today: Darwin actually advocated and encouraged abuse of other races/ethnicities. In *The Descent of Man*, published after *The Origin of Species*, Darwin openly commented on the more significant differences between men of distinct races. For example, Darwin held blacks and Australian Aborigines to be equal to gorillas and then inferred that these would be "done away with" by the "civilised races" in time. He continued:

At some future period, not very distant as measured by centuries, the civilized races of man **will almost certainly exterminate and replace the savage races** throughout the world. At the same time the anthropomorphous apes... will no doubt be exterminated. The break between man in a more civilised state, as we may hope, even than the Caucasian, and some ape as low as baboon, instead of as now between the negro or Australian and the gorilla. [Emphasis added.]

Influential at the highest levels of academia, Darwin unleashed the idea that people who are successful and powerful are thus so because they are innately better. Galton promoted and enshrined the idea within eugenics. Graduating from theory to a socio- cultural movement, eugenics further inculcated and institutionalized racism and White Supremacy. As by-products of Galton's eugenics, new nomenclature and parlance arose to solidify Social Darwinism as a legitimate new cultural movement.

Simply stated: Social Darwinism theorizes that all ethnicities and races are subject to Darwin's theories (including natural selection and the survival of the fittest metaphor). It provided the wealthy and powerful, those in the White Supremacist elitist class, the mechanisms to justify personal delusions of grandeur while perpetuating maltreatment of all others outside of their class structure. Social Darwinists assert human life is in a perpetual struggle for existence. They believed the best way to preserve a "pure" race and lineage while assuring dominion over the looming Malthusian "scarcity of resources" was to subjugate and eliminate all others.

It should be obvious such thinking was and is wholly immoral. Certainly, the Judeo- Christian worldview rejects any such ideas. Such notorious inclinations undermine all humanity. The worst atrocities in human history can be attributed to Social Darwinism; it has been used to justify White Supremacy, slavery, racism, genocide, imperialism, and eugenics.

Darwin Impact on Hitler/Nazi's

Adolf Hitler and the National Socialist German Workers' Party (the "Nazis") provide a powerful and poignant example of what happens when Darwin's theories are embraced and carried out. The Nazis adopted Darwin's playbook of racial classifications. As they embraced Darwin's concept of the "most favored race" in the lineage of "Aryan" supremacy, they unsurprisingly viewed themselves as "Aryans" and thus racially superior. This meant they categorically deemed all others as inferior and therefore "disposable." Aryan superiority was the overarching justification for the Nazi's genocide program.

Nazis considered the Aryan race to be the superior "master race," while they relegated Slavs, Gypsies, and Jews as racially inferior "sub-humans." This meant these other ethnicities would be used for slave labor, lab experiments, and extermination. Nazi propaganda depictions of "pure Aryans" (and associated claims of scientific hierarchy between races) were notions learned and fully embraced because of Darwin's theories.

The known facts and truth about Hitler's connection and embrace of Darwinism are undeniable but also quite inconvenient. Not only interconnected with Darwin's unleashing of racism and White Supremacy, Darwinist enthusiasts are also caught in another conundrum. Undoubtedly, some Darwin apologists will attempt to distance Hitler, his genocidal ambitions to exterminate Jews and the many other Nazi atrocities as somehow separate from Darwinism. The fruit of Nazi ambitions was to divide humanity into race classifications.

What is the pro-Darwin argument strategy? Richard Weikart (Senior Fellow, Center for Science and Culture) has extensively studied and written a number of books exposing Darwin, Hitler and Naziism. Weikart addresses how some Darwin followers attempt to explain away Nazi connections to Darwinism by asserting, "Hitler and Nazi's just used Darwinism as a propaganda tool." Refuting that claim, Weikart writes in his article, "Darwinism in Nazi Propaganda":

It's undeniable, then, that the Nazis employed Darwinism widely in their propaganda efforts. But one might object that the Nazi use of Darwinism was purely a rhetorical strategy: That is, Hitler and other Nazis shrewdly co-opted a dominant scientific paradigm in the service of their insidious political goals. And if there had been another dominant scientific view of origins, they would have claimed that for their cause. There are multiple problems with this objection.

First, it seems to rest on the false assumption that the Nazi regime was primarily opportunistic. Most historians today recognize that Hitler and most leading Nazis were not primarily opportunists but, rather, fanatical ideologues. Sure, Hitler and his comrades were willing to lie to the public if it brought political advantage. However, those lies were always to try to advance their heartfelt ideology, not just to attain power for power's sake.

Second, we have considerable evidence that Hitler and leading Nazis did not just use Darwinism for public consumption, but promoted it in private conversations. It was not just a superficial add-on to gain support for unrelated ideas and policies.

Third, and probably most importantly, this objection fails to recognize that leading Darwinian biologists and anthropologists were promoting scientific racism in the pre-Nazi period. The Nazis were influenced by this scientific racism. Darwinism was an essential part of Nazi racial ideology from the start. It is not like Nazis had their racist ideology in place, and then added Darwinism to the mix to gain more public support. Racism and Darwinism were closely aligned long before the Nazis developed their ideology.

Weikart then draws the following conclusion:

Not only science journals, but also the most important Nazi periodicals, along with pamphlets written to teach the Nazi worldview, all taught the importance of evolutionary biology in Nazi ideology. The authors considered human evolution especially important, because they believed it supported their vision of racial inequality and racial struggle, fundamental parts of the Nazi worldview. No Nazi journal or official Nazi publication (at least, of which I am aware) published articles or essays denying human evolution. However, some did publish essays bashing creationism and anti-evolutionary ideas. Though there was some debate about the exact way that evolution occurred, the version of evolutionary theory most Nazis preferred was the Darwinian theory of natural selection through the struggle for existence.[16]

Knowing that Hitler and the Nazis entirely relied on Darwin's works for motivation for their grotesque disregard for humankind, it's hard to imagine anyone rebutting the obvious connection to eugenics and genocide. After all, his books encouraged eugenics and genocide. Darwin fanned eugenics by writing: *"With savages, the weak in body or mind are soon eliminated"* and: *"We civilized men, on the other hand ... build asylums for the imbecile, the maimed and the sick ... Thus the weak members propagate their kind."*

Further, in *The Descent of Man*, which he published after *The Origin of Species*, frequently equated other (non-Caucasians) ethnicities with animals by writing, *"No one who had attended to the breeding of domestic animals will doubt that this must be highly injurious to the race of man ...Hardly anyone is so ignorant as to allow his worst animals to breed ..."* Clearly, Darwin embraced his racist, White Supremacy and held great disdain for all others. There was no regard or compassion for humanity generally, so his disciples held no regard or any feelings whatsoever as they perpetrated some of the worst horrors and human atrocities in history in the name of Darwinism.[17]

One of the most notorious Nazis in history is Josef Mengele. Mengele was one of Hitler's main henchmen, a German physician and SS captain. "He was the most prominent of a group of Nazi doctors who conducted medical experiments that often- caused great harm or death to the prisoners. In November 1943 Mengele became "Chief Camp Physician" of Auschwitz II (Birkenau). Many of those subjected to Mengele's experiments died as a result or were murdered in order to facilitate post- mortem examination."[18] Mengele was a student of eugenics as, like with most of his contemporaries, he was a firm believer in Darwin-inspired German-race superiority. While he maimed adults in the most heinous ways, Mengele was especially captivated by babies (and especially twin babies); he conducted horrendous child experiments, including taking babies iris' out to simply determine differences in coloration. Unless they were twins, Mengele ordered that all Jewish babies born in Nazi camps to be immediately exterminated. Midwives would deliver the live births, then immediately drown the babies in shallow pails in front of the mothers. Hitler's Nazi camps were camps of unfathomable horrors, with Mengele a reigning monster. "Doctors" like Josef Mengele are perfect examples of how the unleashing of Darwin theories inspired those diabolically inclined to slaughter humanity.

Based on Darwin's theories, Hitler believed the more Jews proliferated, the greater the risk of those he deemed "undesirable" impacting the gene pool of the pure Aryan race. Hitler strategically had his Nazi soldiers to capture them, torture them, and fundamentally eliminate them by controlling all the women and then eliminating their offspring. In Hitler's mind, these grotesque atrocities were wholly justified. Adolf Hitler in *Mein Kampf* unmistakably drew from social Darwinism to state his views, like Darwin's, that the races of humanity could be categorized by strength and fitness:

If reproduction as such is limited and the number of births decreased, then the natural struggle for existence, which only allows the strongest and healthiest to survive, will be replaced by the obvious desire to save at any cost even the weakest and sickest; thereby a progeny is produced, which must become ever more miserable, the longer this mocking of nature and its will persists. . . . A stronger race will supplant the weaker, since the drive for life in its final form will decimate every ridiculous fetter of the so- called humaneness of individuals, in order to make place for the humaneness of nature, which destroys the weak to make place for the strong.[19]

Undoubtedly Hitler took "survival of the fittest" to the extreme. He and the National Socialists had a name for the categories of people who were to be eliminated from Aryan Germany: *untermenschen*, meaning "sub-humans." It was another Hitler comrade, Nazi Party member Ernst Rüdin, one of the "fathers" of racial hygiene, who advocated eliminating all those with hereditary defects – "untermensch" – from the human gene pool. Rüdin's policy goal led to millions dying in the Holocaust because he summarily classified all Jews as sub-human. It may be hard to imagine, but Adolf Hitler provides just one classic example of what happens when Darwinism is embraced: It spawns racism, "White Supremacy" and eugenics. Sadly, Hitler was not alone. There were many more who took Darwin's theories into their wretched souls.

Hitler and the Nazi Party exemplify what happens under the auspices of firmly embracing Darwinian ideologies. Nazis implemented "Social Darwinism" on a large scale, following a fundamental tenet of Social Darwinism, "scientific racism." As we've seen especially in the 20th and 21st centuries, anything claiming to be "scientific" receives at least respectful consideration and often blind acceptance. To this very day, Darwinism-based scientific racism still rages around the globe. As we will see, Hitler was just one of many wretched reprobates greatly impacted by Darwin.

Darwinian Influence on Genocidal Despots

Not restricted to Hitler, Darwin profoundly influenced Vladimir Lenin, Joseph Stalin, Mao Zedong, Pol Pot, Nicolae Ceaușescu, Kim Il Sung, Margaret Sanger, Karl Marx and Friedrich Engels, and others whose eugenic policies and totalitarian regimes aborted, killed and enslaved millions. Darwin greatly influenced Joseph Stalin, as recounted in *Landmarks in the Life of Stalin* (1942): "At a very early age, while still a pupil in the ecclesiastical school, Comrade Stalin developed a critical mind and revolutionary sentiments. He began to read Darwin and became an atheist." Once his respect for God and humanity was fully undermined and debased by his zealous embrace Darwinism, Stalin used intentional famines, forced labor and executions to eliminate over 7 million Ukrainians. Stalin's notorious 1937 order No. 00447 called for the mass execution and exile of "socially harmful elements" as "enemies of the people." Estimates of deaths during the Stalinist period range from 8 to 61 million. Stalin's fervency for Darwin underlaid many of his actions and policies. Stalin himself stated the Soviet state- controlled "common core" type indoctrination: "There are three things that we do to disabuse the minds of our seminary students. We had to teach them the age of the earth, the geologic origin, and Darwin's teachings."

Mao Zedong also expressly stood upon Darwinism to guide his actions. Of Darwin, Mao stated: "Chinese socialism is founded upon Darwin and the theory of evolution."[20] Michael Pitman wrote in *Adam and Evolution* (London, England: Rider & Co., 1984, 24): "After 1949 when the communists took control of China, the first new text introduced to all the schools was neither Marxist nor Leninist, but Darwinian." Mao's Darwinism- motivated Communist Party policies resulted in an estimated 80 million deaths.[21]

Pol Pot's communist Khmer Rouge regime killed two million Cambodians in his "killing fields" between 1975 and 1979. With Darwinist-utilitarian logic, Pol Pot pithily stated: "Keeping you is no gain. Losing you is no loss."

In the article "Nationalism in the Slave States of Soviet Russia, Nazi Germany and now, China" (Dec. 23, 2010),

Lev Navrozov, an immigrant from the U.S.S.R. who worked with the Center for the Survival of Western Democracies, stated:

Once upon a time it was assumed that a slave should fulfill the slave- owners' order as efficiently as a machine. But after Stalin, Hitler, and Mao ... slaves must relive the order, and hence scream in their delight to kill and be killed.

Notably, in 1948 George Orwell described this same concept of the new age of totalitarianism in his dystopic novel, *1984*.

It has been estimated over 100 million innocent lives have been lost due to grotesque human atrocities committed under direct influence of Darwin's ideologies.[22] Think about it: Over one hundred million innocent souls were mercilessly murdered. According to some estimates, if you combine that 100 million souls with the number of deaths from every war that has been fought in human history, you would end up with between 150 million to 1 billion. These numbers are staggering and humanly unfathomable. Yet those deaths, while horrendous, don't come anywhere near the number of innocent children brazenly killed in the most horrific ways in just the past 50 years: an estimated 1.5 to 2 billion children being eliminated.[23]

Such human carnage is astonishing! How can it be that the number of babies killed far surpasses the number of all human atrocities at the hands of the worst despots, and including all war deaths, from the beginning of time? The fundamental ideas of eugenics and Social Darwinism gave rise to the worldwide and continuing wave of abortion.

The unleashing of Darwin and Galton's eugenics theories inspired a hateful, racist, KKK-loving, White supremacist named Margret Sanger. Sanger loomed large in the eugenics movement, with her works and legacy ongoing and even celebrated by supporters to this day.

Margret Sanger's record and account confirm her depth of Darwinistic delusions and her contorted and contrived heart full of hatred. Sanger's despicable acts include her actively participating as a keynote speaker for the women's KKK rallies. Sanger was a frequent honored guest at Democrat-led KKK events and ceremonies. Sanger's track- record of inspiring death and destruction is long. Her writings and commentaries are notorious and cannot be excused. Consider some of Sanger's direct quotes:

- "[We] are paying for and even submitting to the dictates of an ever-increasing, unceasingly spawning class of human beings who never should have been born at all"[24]

- "The most merciful thing that a large family does to one of its members is to kill it."[25]

- "We don't want the word to get out that we want to exterminate the Negro population"- Margaret Sanger

- The purpose of birth control was "to create a race of thoroughbreds."[26]

- Birth control must ultimately lead to a cleaner race."[27]

- [Referring to Blacks and other disfavored people as] "human weeds," "reckless breeders," "unfit," "feeble-minded," and "undesirables"

- [On the rights of the handicapped and mentally ill, and racial minorities:] "more children from the fit, less from the unfit—that is the chief aim of birth control."[28]

- "Blacks and Jews are a menace to the race…We must prevent multiplication of this bad stock…."

- "The lower down in the scale of human development we go the less sexual control we

- find. It is said the aboriginal Australian, the lowest known species of the human family, just a step higher than the chimpanzee in brain development."[29]

The above-listed examples are just some of Sanger's many comments confirming her fervent Darwinist embrace and racist hate. Many more blatantly and horribly evil written quotes from Sanger exist, and one can only imagine how Sanger spoke when her words weren't written down.[30]

Darwin's theme of *"most favored races,"* and his role in unleashing eugenics, indisputably influenced Margaret Sanger, as she was a huge promoter of "eugenics" and "forced sterilization" to eliminate inferior races. In 1921, Sanger founded a non- profit organization, the American Birth Control League, which became Planned Parenthood to help carry out her scheme to "exterminate negroes."[31]

Publicly-available reports show Planned Parenthood aborts over 300,000 babies a year, totaling over 7 million since abortion was legalized in 1973.[32] Margret Sangers' disgusting racist schemes were wholly motivated by her die-hard eugenicist goals. Planned Parenthood was and is the edifice to fully carry out her diabolical plans to exterminate those not meeting "pure Aryan" genealogy (read, those not White). Sanger intensely loathed and disdained Blacks. The well-documented facts explain Sanger and Planned Parenthood's programs to target and actively eliminate Blacks and Hispanics that are being carried out to this very day.

Margaret Sanger confirmed her racial hatred of Blacks while speaking at the Women's KKK rallies. Margaret Sanger wrote in her autobiography that she addressed a Ku Klux Klan rally in Silver Lake, New Jersey in 1938.

Quoted in "Apostle of Birth Control Sees Cause Gaining Here" (*The New York Times*, April 8, 1923, p. xii):

Birth control is not contraception indiscriminately and thoughtlessly practiced. It means the release and cultivation of the better racial elements in our society, and the gradual suppression, elimination and eventual extirpation of defective stocks — those human weeds which threaten the blooming of the finest flowers of American civilization.

In a radio interview on WFAB Syracuse, February 2, 1924 ("The Meaning of Birth Control," April 1924, p. 111): Sanger stated:

Just think for a moment of the meaning of the word kindergarten — a garden of children ... Every expert gardener ... knows that no plant would have a fair chance of life if it were overcrowded or choked by weeds ... If plants, and live stock as well, require space and air, sunlight and love, children need them even more ... A farmer would rather produce a thousand thoroughbreds than a million runts. How are we to breed a race of human thoroughbreds unless we follow the same plan? We must make this country into a garden of children instead of a disorderly back lot overrun with human weeds.

In her address to the New History Society, New York City, January 1, 1932, Sanger summarized in "A Plan for Peace," April 1932, pp. 107-108:

Keep the doors of immigration closed to the entrance of certain aliens whose condition is known to be detrimental to the stamina of the race, such as feebleminded, idiots, morons, insane, syphilitic, epileptic, criminal, professional prostitutes, and others in this class barred by the immigration laws of 1924 ...Apply a stern and rigid policy of sterilization and segregation to that grade of population whose progeny is tainted, or whose inheritance is such that objectionable traits may be transmitted to offspring ...Insure the country against future burdens of maintenance for numerous offspring as may be born of feeble-minded parents, by pensioning all persons with transmissible disease who voluntarily consent to sterilization ...Give certain dysgenic groups in our population their choice of segregation or sterilization.

These statements confirm Sanger's xenophobia and strict adherence to "scientific" Darwinism. These evil sentiments alone don't tell the whole story.

Sanger also spread and unleashed her racist hate through her writings. In *Pivot of Civilization* (1922, ch. 12, "Woman and the Future"), Sanger wrote:

We are informed that the psychological examination of the drafted men indicated that nearly half - 47.3 per cent. - of the population had the mentality of twelve-year-old children or less - in other words that they are morons ...Our 'overhead' expense in segregating the delinquent, the defective and the dependent, in prisons, asylums and permanent homes, our failure to segregate morons who are increasing and multiplying ... demonstrate our foolhardy and extravagant sentimentalism. No industrial corporation could maintain its existence upon such a foundation. Yet hardheaded 'captains of industry,' financiers who pride themselves upon their cool-headed and keen-sighted business ability are dropping millions into rosewater philanthropies and charities that are silly at best and vicious at worst.

Sanger was so angry about other ethnicities infringing on her "superior" race and class, she felt it necessary to do more than just talk about the tenets of eugenics, she felt impelled to take action. In her mind, this meant there was a need to "exterminate!"

As quoted above, Sanger called Blacks "reckless breeders" and "weeds that need to be eliminated," while notoriously proclaiming, "We don't want the word to go out that we want to eliminate the Negro population!" Sanger's infamously hateful legacy continues to this day as Planned Parenthood continues to disproportionally target Black and Brown populations by strategically placing clinics primarily in urban areas. Considering Blacks make up only about 13% of population and women of child-bearing ages making up about one-fourth of that (approx. 3%), Planned Parenthood has conveniently situated an overwhelming percentage of its "abortuaries" (60-80% by some estimates) to cater to this specific market, a very small percentage of the overall female market. Sanger's schemes to "eliminate Blacks" via Planned Parenthood's targeting of Black communities have resulted in the Black baby deaths making up approx. 40% of all abortions while representing only 3% of the women demographics; disproportional gratuitous Black genocide has resulted.[33]

Eugenics and the U.S. Supreme Court

There are countless Sanger and Planned Parenthood defenders. Many will attempt to gloss over the fact the movement was started with the full intent of spreading eugenics, and has been all about facilitating the murder by Blacks, Hispanics and other non- Caucasian minorities of their babies thereby diminishing the growth of those "undesirable elements" in our society. Even Supreme Court Justice Ruth Bader Ginsburg recognized what abortion was *really* all about. Ginsburg was quoted in the *New York Times Magazine*: "Frankly I had thought that at the time (*Roe v. Wade*) was decided," that "there was concern about population growth and particularly growth in populations that *we don't want to have too many of.*"

Excuse me?! Ginsburg knew all along that abortion was really all about Darwin's scientific racism propagated through eugenics. Yet, she ruled in favor of every pro-abortion case that reached the Supreme Court. Fortunately, the Supreme Court has experienced dramatic change recently, and changes in America's systemically embracing scientific racism might possibly end soon.

One of Ginsburg's colleagues on the Supreme Court is Constitutional stalwart Clarence Thomas. Justice Thomas has much to say about the duplicitously diabolical evils of Planned Parenthood and abortion. In the case *Box v. Planned Parenthood of Indiana and Kentucky* (concurring opinion, May 28, 2019),[34] Justice Thomas wrote:

Planned Parenthood founder Margaret Sanger was particularly open about the fact that birth control could be used for eugenic purposes ...Like many elites of her day, Sanger accepted that eugenics was "the most adequate and thorough avenue to the solution of racial, political and social problems" ... In her view, birth-control advocates and eugenicists were "seeking a single end" "to assist the race toward the elimination of the unfit"' ...

Justice Thomas continued:

Sanger herself campaigned for birth control in black communities. In 1930, she opened a birth-control clinic in Harlem ... In 1939, Sanger initiated the "Negro Project," an effort to promote birth control in poor, Southern black communities ...In a report titled "Birth Control and the Negro," Sanger and her coauthors identified blacks as "the great problem of the South" ... and developed a birth-control program geared toward this population. She later emphasized that black ministers should be involved in the program, noting, "We do not want word to go out that we want to exterminate the Negro population, and the minister is the man who can straighten out that idea if it ever occurs to any of their more rebellious members."

When you connect the dots of history and facts beginning with the racism and White Supremacy unleashed by Darwin and his followers, an indisputably sickening pattern of human debasement emerges. Darwinian theories and writings are the "root" of a rampage of evils that brought forth the "fruit" of merciless atrocities inflicted upon innocents worldwide. The most heinous atrocities in human history began with Darwin's ranking of humans, which led to Galton's starting and unleashing eugenics, which led to the eugenics movement, which led to atrocities of Hitler and Mengele, which led to eugenics advocate Margret Sanger, which led to the founding of Planned Parenthood, which has led to White Supremacist/racially motivated disproportional murder of innocent Black babies, which has led to the continued brazen murder of approximately 50 million innocent unborn babies in the U.S., and results in approximately 1-1.5 billion unborn babies murdered worldwide! The heartbreaking dots are connected: Darwin and his followers unleashed an unparalleled level of evil that continues unabated to this day.

A thoughtful observer of the revealed facts and connections could raise poignant and quite "inconvenient" questions, such as:

- *With the full understanding that eugenics had nothing to do with "women's health," and was specifically created by Darwin and Galton as a racist scheme to exterminate all other ethnicities (i.e., non-white), is there any logical way people can assert pure motives and justification for supporting eugenics and Planned Parenthood going forward? Do you have any doubt eugenics is manifestly racist, and Planned Parenthood was started in order to expedite overlaying the racist scheme of "extermination" targeted at Black communities?*

- *How could anyone assert they utterly disdain Hitler and his atrocities while at the same time lauding, honoring and revering Margaret Sanger? The two harbored the same mindset, yet on balance, hasn't Sanger directly precipitated many more killings of innocents than Hitler?*

- *Keeping their respective backgrounds in mind, how can anyone boast about gleefully supporting Margaret Sanger and Planned Parenthood?*

- *By literal definition, isn't Planned Parenthood a good example of a systematically racist organization?*

- *Given that Sanger started Planned Parenthood with the sole mission to "exterminate the negro population" (her words), how can anyone attempt to continue supporting Planned Parenthood by sticking to the tired mantra of "woman's right to choose?" This mantra merely conceals Planned Parenthood's foundational mission of exterminating Blacks!*

- *If, after learning of these facts, people continue diehard support of Planned Parenthood, wouldn't they fit the definition of a racist and White Supremacist? (Keep in mind, in today's "cancel culture," if you even tangentially support a "racist," you're automatically deemed a confirmed racist yourself.)*

Up to this point, much has been uncovered, illuminated and connected directly to the "root" of racism and White Supremacy. Still, this root runs very deep; the taproot needs to be further exposed, then uprooted.

The great missionary Mother Theresa fully understood how Darwinism, eugenics, and abortion are evil scourges hatched by diabolical schemes directly from the pits of hell. A famous quote confirming her disdain for killing innocent babies is: *"A nation that kills its children in the womb has lost its soul" ~ Mother Theresa*

You getting "WOKEd Up?"

CHAPTER FIVE
"WOKESTERS OF THE WORLD, UNITE!"
INTERSECTION OF SOCIAL DARWINISM AND MARXISM

"A lie doesn't become truth, wrong doesn't become right, and evil doesn't become good, just because it's accepted by a majority."

~ Booker T. Washington

One of Darwin's most significant disciples is Karl Marx. To this day, Karl Marx and his social and economic theories continue to dominate with a profound effect on the world.

Karl Marx is known for the slogan, "Workers of the world, unite!" For generations, this has been the rallying cry in the rise and revolution of the "working-class" poor worldwide. Ironically, this generations-old cry has morphed from "Workers of the world, unite" to "*wokesters* of the world, unite!" The transformation in language caused a transition from a mostly *economic* cry for "workers," to a mostly *cultural* cry for "wokesters." The "root" of these movements (notably Karl Marx) and end goals (notably "revolution") are the same, but the tactics have been adjusted to reflect global socio/cultural worldviews.

To casual observers, the historical origins and emergence of wokeism may seem to be "organic" manifestations of the rigors and woes of modern times. However, after reading this chapter, if you remember nothing else, remember this: *While it seems wokeism and being woke are new, they are not!*

Wokeism may be "trendy," but it is not new. The emergence of wokeism is not viral, opportunistic, or "purely organic." It is *by design*. Under the guise of other social labels, wokeism has been building for millennia. What are the roots of wokeism? Why has it gained so much notoriety and momentum? If news, commentary, public statements and social media are any indication, wokeism definitely has cultural and historical significance. To prevent blindly being gripped and swept into this new trend, it's worthwhile to identify its historical roots and foundations.

Wokeism's roots go back to ancient history, starting with Plato. In 379 BC, Plato wrote *Republic*. Heralded as a great work in political philosophy, *Republic* provided a philosophical picture of utopia (a place of perfection), much of which relies on political elites (and "masterminds") to oversee and provide for "the masses." Building on Plato's work to present a variation of the same theme was Thomas More's *Utopia* (1516). While *Utopia* was purely fictional, it gave ideas and concepts built on Plato's *Republic*, painting a picture of the masses experiencing utopia under the oversight and governance of political "masterminds."

Then, in 1651, *Leviathan* was written by Thomas Hobbes. *Leviathan* presented another variation of the theme of ideas in Republic and Utopia. Hobbes perpetuated the idea that a body of "sovereigns," notably political masterminds, need to oversee the commonwealth of the masses.

This common paradigm creates obvious conflict within itself because the masterminds all want to remain masters, and everyone else wants to ascend also to become masters. (The masters hold all the power and influence). Obviously, this paradigm only infuses more chaos, hatred, and divisions – it does not increase unity! For people seeking individual liberty and social harmony, the ancient political philosophers' assertions and paradigms promising utopia are unworkable and tremendously flawed.

Ancient Philosophy of Wokeism

The philosophers who shared the common view that an elite class of masterminds should run societies also fundamentally rejected the notion of governments being held accountable and restricted by the guardrails of what we would today call a representative democratic republic. The ancient thinkers' works ignored the fact that human beings are horribly flawed. Humans are not innately "good"; human nature includes evil potentials and tendencies. Therefore, expecting sincere altruistically- motivated leaders ("the sovereign") to benevolently oversee the masses ("the governed") has been found throughout history to be an impossibility. Chaos, distrust, irreparable societal divisions and mass death are just some of the notable outcomes of these utopian dreams. All utopian ideologies pushing for "the sovereign" elites to rule over a powerless mass citizenry are untenable for free societies.

While the writings of Plato, More and Hobbes are great sources for intellectual discussions on political philosophy, many people with nefarious intent have taken these fictional (even dystopian) works to heart. There has been a constant, persistent push toward global governance via totalitarian masterminds for generations. Ultimately, this effort has led to an embrace of Karl Marx and Marxism and, ultimately, our current era of wokeism. After connecting the dots with history, we'll see that our current socio/political climate is a direct culmination of ancient political philosophies of utopian- themed works of fiction.

"Wokesters" reject Capitalism and gleefully tout Marxism. That said, wokeism can generally be described as a neo-

Marxist movement that inculcates aspects of all the other preceding utopian visions, and culminates with Social Darwinism (i.e., Darwinian ideologies infused in and through modern culture). Social Darwinism is undergirded with Darwinian sentiments of: (1) race/class superiority, "survival of the fittest"—the idea that certain people become powerful in society because they are innately better; and (2) eugenics. Ironically, while wokesters unite purportedly to fight racism, they embrace roots of Social Darwinism that firmly instantiates (not rejects) racism.

Specifically, Darwinism and all its derivatives and compatible theories like Marxism, rely on scientific racism (eugenics) to feed their demented need to exert superiority over others. Whether ignorant of these facts or not, many "wokesters" view wokeism as "a dream come true!" They blindly push toward a "woke revolution" as a way to overturn "patriarchy," meritocracy, civil society, and all existing social order. Downstream consequences and outcomes of their revolution are scarcely considered. Vladimir Lenin, the initial ruler of the Union of Soviet Socialist Republics (USSR), deemed an apropos cliché for such true believers (those who refuse to connect the dots" and fervently follow ideology "just because"); Lenin deemed them "useful idiots." On this one point, I agree with Lenin...useful idiots indeed!

Fundamentally, wokeism uses cultural forces ("cancel culture," censoring, shaming, doxing, guilting, race-baiting, corporate "shake downs" and myriad other socially constructed abuses) as cudgels to drain the souls of the people in order to transform *individuals* into meek, fully compliant and obedient worshippers of the *collective*. In all the above-described political-philosophical visions, from Plato through Hobbes, utopia requires a compliant citizenry to humbly bow to sovereign, mastermind elites who oversee the *collective* from the perspective of a global commonwealth. The ultimate goal is to firmly instantiate global governments (and governance) as the "masterminds" oversee wholly compliant "plebs."

Social Darwinism

Until now, the major roadblock to the ultimate goal has been: "How do you get 'free people' to give up their 'liberties' and submit themselves to globalist masterminds?" This is the same problem facing the designs of Karl Marx and Marxism. The evolution and transitionary stages from Darwinian theories, to Social Darwinism, to Cultural Marxism, and now to modern-day "wokeism," have been subtle. Mostly the changes appear as just semantics and linguistics aiming to reflect shifting cultural paradigms. Foundationally, however, Darwinism and Marxism undergird wokeism. Having explored the essentials of Darwin's theories as they pertain to race, we can now to turn to better understanding and interpreting Karl Marx.

Recognizing the dots connecting historical facts and truths about Darwin's role in unleashing institutionalized and scientific rationalizations for racism and White supremacy, we realize that only the most hateful, debased, and demented types of personalities are seduced to fully embrace his theories. Karl Marx is perhaps the best example of this personality. He took Darwin's naturalist/materialist notions to heart and unleashed a confluence of Darwinism coupled with utopian dreams of ancient political philosophers to culminate in what we call today "being woke" (or "cultural Marxism"). However, as you awaken to the realities, you'll recognize that the notion of woke is more like "a joke due to noted ironies." This becomes clearer when uncovering and more fully assessing the sordid and wholly diabolical background and history of Karl Marx.

Recall the irony of the completely opposite forces of two men, Abraham Lincoln and Charles Darwin, being born in the same year – the same is true of the powerful diametric forces of Karl Marx and Frederick Douglass. Both men were born in 1818, but there the similarities end. Marx hated God and boasted his ultimate goal in life was to "dethrone God." Douglass, on the other hand, loved God, believed God divinely provided for him, and desired to serve Him by becoming an ordained minister.

Marx was born "privileged" and elitist, so he was referred to as lazy while he audaciously raged against capitalism. Douglass, on the other hand, was born into slavery, worked hard every day of his life and (out of his love for capitalism) became a successful entrepreneur. Marx died angrily, embracing unforgiveness toward those he thought didn't do enough to financially support him, while Douglass was so committed to repentance and forgiveness, he went out of his way to find and forgive his past enslavers. To this day, Marx and Douglass have left indelible marks on humanity. Their respective ideologies live on as their legacy serves as great reminders and examples; truly, both legacies still exert profound influence in individual lives, and in culture and societies worldwide. But again, they held wholly diametric views, and the only *one thing* they shared in common was the year they were born.

Loathsome Marx

Karl Marx was born to a Jewish family on May 5, 1818. At an early age Marx rejected God, the notion of God or any Supreme Being. He went to college, but was characterized as a lazy, "unserious" student. As seems typical of elitist students, Marx wholly relied on his parents' financial support instead of working. Marx never had a real job during his lifetime and was a serial grifter, quite happy to live by mooching off friends and family. Although Marx would assert "workers' rights," he failed to live up to his own convictions. As historian Paul Johnson explained in his book, *Intellectuals* (1988): *"in his own household ... Helen Demuth [the life-long family maid]. She got her keep but was paid nothing ... She was a ferociously hard worker, not only cleaning and scrubbing, but managing the family budget ... Marx never paid her a penny ...In 1849-50 ... [Helen] became Marx's mistress and conceived a child ... Marx refused to acknowledge his responsibility, then or ever, and flatly denied the rumors that he was the father... [The son] was put out to be fostered by a working-class family called Lewis but allowed to visit the Marx household [to see his mother]. He was, however, forbidden to use the front door and obliged to see his mother only in the kitchen.*

Marx was terrified that [the boy's] paternity would be discovered and that this would do him fatal damage as a revolutionary leader and seer ... [Marx] persuaded Engels to acknowledge [the boy] privately, as a cover story for family consumption. But Engels ... was not willing to take the secret to the grave. Engels died, of cancer of the throat, on 5 August 1895; unable to speak but unwilling that Eleanor [one of Marx's daughters] should continue to think her father unsullied, he wrote on a slate: 'Freddy [the boy's name] is Marx's son ..." [35]

To summarize, Marx was the ultimate pathetic and loathsome soul. He had a live-in maid that worked hard for him and his family (literally "slaving") for years, but he never paid her a penny. He summarily used his her as a sex slave; she was his live-in maid for sex. Marx had "on-demand" adulterous sex with his maid and this sordid affair eventually bore him an illegitimate child. But Fredrick

Engels, his longtime financial and intellectual collaborator, claimed the child to save Marx from embarrassment and social fallout that would've surely ensued based on his unconscionable adulterous actions.

Marx was a wretchedly disgusting human being deserving of disdain. Marx is certainly not the kind of person that deserves admiration and respect. The disgust for Marx is based on his social interactions and deeds and his physical being. For decades, Marx suffered with debilitating boils (festering and painful) which covered most of body. As a result, he was known to carry a stench of horrible body odor and was known to not bathe or groom. Fundamentally, Marx's stature (physically and emotionally) was that of a madman.

Karl Marx's friends described him as being wretched, tormented, and demonically possessed. His habitus was restless and indicative of a ragingly demented demoniac. Marx's closest friend and collaborator, Frederick Engels, referred to Karl Marx as being possessed, a "monster of ten thousand devils!"[36] Marx's biographer Robert Payne who wrote, *"There were times when Marx seemed to be possessed by demons. He had the devil's view of the world and the devil's malignity. Sometimes Marx seemed to know that he was accomplishing works of evil."* What sparked this level of virulent hate and disdain for God, and full embrace of demonic evil? All of the origins may not be known, but Darwinism cemented his worldview.

Darwin's Impact on Karl Marx

Marx's political philosophies were born of aggrievement for his pathetic life and his avowed commitment to following Darwin and his theories. Darwin's *Origin of Species* was read, reread, and had a major ideological influence on Karl

Marx. Marx saw "survival of the fittest" as validating his "dialectical conflict," where labor and community organizers would create domestic chaos to enable communist dictators to usurp power. Karl Marx wrote to Lassalle, January 16, 1861: *"Darwin's book is very important and serves me as a basis in natural selection for the class struggle in history."*[37]

Additionally, Marx dedicated a personal copy his book, *Das Kapital*, to Charles Darwin, inscribing that he was a "sincere admirer" of Darwin. When Darwin's theories, again fully encompassing anti-God theories on creation while offering "justification" for scientific racism, are overlayed and coupled with perpetual aggrievement and discontent, a "monster" like Marx can easily emerge.

We can surmise that if Darwin hadn't existed, there would not have been an unleashing of social distinctions (and associated parlance) to produce a "superiority complex" and justification for scientific racism and White Supremacy. In that case, Karl Marx and his notorious works would likely have not matured and flourished. But, since Darwin did exist and had such an incredible influence on Marx, Marx's works were unleashed and ultimately to plague humanity. As a result of Marx, humanity has witnessed the acceleration of unbridled demonism.

You don't need deep knowledge of history to see it. Most Marxists I encounter today demonstrate the same level of elitist demonism of Karl Marx; they're wholly discontent, lazy and wretched as well. Notably, Marx's despicable temperament was not just toward those he knew, he seemed to hate everyone. Especially Blacks! Just as much as Karl Marx was virulently hateful of God, he was equally hateful of Blacks and other ethnicities. Marx was wholly cruel and often ridiculed those he disagreed with. He often used insults and racist slurs when ridiculing others.

Marx's Racism

In an 1862 letter to Frederick Engels, Marx described leading nineteenth-century German socialist, Ferdinand Lassalle, in the following way:

The Jewish Nigger Lassalle ... fortunately departs at the end of this week ... It is now absolutely clear to me that, as both the shape of his head and his hair texture shows – he descends from the Negros who joined Moses' flight from Egypt (unless his mother or grandmother on the paternal side hybridized with a nigger). Now this combination of Germanness and Jewishness with a primarily Negro substance creates a strange product. The pushiness of the fellow is also nigger-like.[38]

Marx's racism was just as hideous and grotesque as his physical appearance; it was boundless! Though he was of Jewish descent, Marx characterized Jews as follows: the "worldly religion" of Jews was "huckstering." Erik van Ree, a lecturer at the Institute for East European Studies of the University of Amsterdam, wrote of Marx and Engel's racism in a paper for the *Journal of Political Ideologies*. He explained how racial classifications and explanations of economic development were components of early Marxist thought:

In Marx and Engels's understanding, racial disparities emerged under the influence of shared natural and social conditions hardening into heredity and of the mixing of blood. They racialized skin-color groups, ethnicities, nations, and social classes, while endowing them with innate superior and inferior character traits. They regarded race as part of humanity's natural conditions, upon which the production system rested. 'Races' endowed with superior qualities would boost economic development and productivity, while the less endowed ones would hold humanity back. Importantly, van Ree concluded that Marx and Engels' statements on race went beyond "unthinkingly repeating the stereotypes and prejudices of the day. "[39]

These insights readily confirm Darwin's racist, supremacist influence on Marx.

Marx was driven by race distinctions. He consistently degraded all ethnicities other than the "pure" Aryan race (White Supremacy). When the U.S. annexed California after the Mexican-American War, Marx wrote: "Without violence nothing is ever accomplished in history." Then he asked, *"Is it a misfortune that magnificent California was seized from the lazy Mexicans who did not know what to do with it?" Friedrich Engels added: "In America we have witnessed the conquest of Mexico and have rejoiced at it. It is to the interest of its own development that Mexico will be placed under the tutelage of the United States. "*

Many of Marx's racist ideas were reported in *Karl Marx, Racist* a book written by Nathaniel Weyl, a former member of the U.S. Communist Party. In 1887, Paul Lafargue, Marx's son-in-law, was a candidate for a council seat in a Paris district that contained a zoo. Engels claimed that Paul had "one eighth or one twelfth nigger blood." In an April 1887 letter to Paul's wife, Engels wrote, *"Being in his quality as a nigger, a degree nearer to the rest of the animal kingdom than the rest of us, he is undoubtedly the most appropriate representative of that district."*

Darwin's ugly racism and White Supremacy was indeed deep-rooted within Marx and Engels. And they were proud of it! So proud in fact, through his racist rants, Marx seemed to have passed along his grotesque racism to his daughters. Marx's daughter, Jenney, once flippantly complained to her sister Eleanor that, "I drudge like a nigger." When one of Marx's daughters married a Cuban man, Marx notoriously considered him as "being marred by negro blood in his veins." He further denigrated him by referring to him as "negrillo" and "the gorilla." He would complain to Engels that his son-in-law "has the blemish customarily found in the negro tribe- no sense of shame, by this I mean making a fool of oneself."[40] Pretty obviously Marx was a diehard racist. He embraced the Darwinist "superiority complex" and felt justified in minimizing and ignoring the plight of Blacks as they fought to be recognized as equals...indeed even as "human."

Marx and Engels heard of the many atrocities against Blacks during the time of slavery in the U.S., but they had zero sensitivity or compassion for it. Based on his embrace of Darwinist ideology, Marx surely felt slaves were duly inferior. While slavery reigned, his only sensitivity and effort was directed toward his schemes for a revolution with the "working-class" poor.

Unlike the honorable Frederick Douglass who fought for civil and human rights for slaves in the U.S., the contemptible Marx wholly ignored this scourge; he felt "workers" (proletariat) were much worse off than slaves. Since he held disdain for Blacks, he felt their plight was justified (via scientific racism), Marx therefore had no serious concerns about the atrocities of slavery. Marx's selfish ambitions to succeed in his utopian dreams for revolution kept him strictly focused on the task of uniting workers of the world against the "bourgeoisie."

In Marx's mind, the Jew in bourgeois society captured the essence of everything he considered despicable in the capitalist system, and only with the end of the capitalist system would there be an end to most of those unattractive qualities. Here is Marx's conception of the Jewish mind in nineteenth-century Europe, from his essay "On the Jewish Question" (1844):

What is the secular basis of Judaism? Practical need, self-interest. What is the worldly cult of the Jew? Haggling. What is his worldly god? Money! ... Money is the jealous god of Israel before whom no other god may exist. Money degrades all the gods of mankind and converts them into commodities ... What is contained abstractly in the Jewish religion – contempt for theory, for art, for history, for man as an end in himself ... The social emancipation of the Jew is the emancipation of society from Jewishness.[41]

(Marx's caricaturing description of the asserted "Jewish mindset" rings amazingly similar to those that were later written by the Nazi "race-scientists" of the 1930s, who also condemned Jews for the same self-interested pursuit of money and the resulting degenerative influence they believed Jews had upon the German people.)

Marx's Ultimate Goal

Marx's ultimate goal was to compete with and "dethrone God." He virulently hated God, and even the notion of God. His motivation to start the Communist movement was to overthrow the existing social order, while undermining religions and faith. Marx envisioned reorienting human nature with Communism occupying "the center of the universe" for every individual. To eventually arrive to the point of mass adoption of Communism, Marx knew he would have to instill chaos and division to drive toward an eventual "revolution." Marx anticipated that persistent social discord would eventually overthrow the prevailing social order.

To agitate the masses, he encouraged criticizing of everything. In a letter to Arnold Ruge, Marx stated, "the *ruthless criticism of the existing order*, ruthless in that it will shrink neither from its own discoveries nor from conflict

73

with the powers that be." He pushed for the ruthless and unceasing criticism of all that exists. Wokesters of the world today in fact unite around this same principle of insatiably criticizing all existing social order.

The criticism from wokesters is relentless. If you are a business owner, wokesters criticize you by asserting, "you didn't build that!" "Our *collective* afforded you the ability to succeed, therefore you owe us! You must 'pay your fair share!'"

Suppose you're a White Christian male and father. In that case, you are criticized by summarily being deemed part of the "American patriarchy." Therefore, you're a White Supremacist and racist (even though Wokeish ideology was borne out of Darwin and Marx, who were definitively racist and White Supremacist).

If you are a free-thinking Black person who fully observes the brainwashing and duplicitous false narratives, and therefore you reject the racism of Darwin, Marx, and eugenics of Planned Parenthood, then you are criticized as "White passing," having "internalized racism" or myriad other pejoratives.

Suppose you are a White (male or female). In that case, you are mercilessly criticized because your supposed ignorance of "White privilege" and therefore must experience the guilt and shame of what has happened to Blacks of generations past (notably during slavery).

All of these relentless critiques are purposeful. The purposefulness is most obvious with the advent of Critical Race Theory (CRT). CRT is the "wokesters'" tool to bludgeon all dissenters, and to force compliance with an inevitable Marxist structure that upends all existing social order (family structure, career/job, capitalistic economic foundations, and faith/religion) in pursuit of ultimately bringing forth the communist utopia Marx envisioned.

Ronald Reagan once described a communist as one who reads Karl Marx, and an "anti- communist" a one who understands Karl Marx. That's a profound statement. In the same vein, I'd add (with the focus on racism and White Supremacy): A racist and White Supremacist is one who reads and understands Charles Darwin/Darwinism, and nevertheless fervently supports and embraces any forms of Marxism. While these statements are personal observations, they are not to be dismissed as shallow insults or untrue; they should be regarded with all seriousness because they are factually grounded. The fact is, unless you are a brainwashed adolescent with marginal intelligence, it is not a "badge of honor" to affirm an avowed allegiance to Marxism. On the contrary, it's confirmation of abject buffoonery.

Seriously: Who would gleefully attest to being a disciple of demonism? When "Cultural Marxism" is borne out of the *roots* of social Darwinism, and the *roots* of racism and White Supremacy are the obvious inescapable *fruit* of these diabolical ideologies, then how can prophets of wokeism somehow assert that embracing the racist-Darwinist-eugenicist complex allows them to be enlightened and "anti-racist?"

Moreover, how can avid followers of a lazy, never-having-worked, slave-driving (literally), hate-filled moocher like Marx, claim his pathetic ideologies are better than those participating in free-markets? Marx has much in common with the KKK and White Supremacist groups of today (anti-Semitic, manifest hatred of Blacks and Latinos, embrace of demonic roots of "natural selection" and eugenics, etc.). So how can any person or institution proclaim fervency for Marxism while purportedly standing against racism and White Supremacy? *Vibe on Internal contradiction much?* Wokeism, in its current cultural context, is duplicitous, unserious and nonsensical.

With the myriad well-documented insidious actions and deeds (including maiming and killing of 1 billion+ innocent) committed under the auspices of Marx, Marxism, Cultural Marxism, and now wokeism, how has it been surviving and thriving over the many decades? How have Marx's personal history and deeds been ceremoniously covered up to the extent we now face a global threat of rampaging Marxism (under the auspices of One World Order, World Economic Forum/World Economic Council, Council of Foreign Relations and etc.) and fulfillment of Marx's utopian dreams? We can see clearly: Marxism survives because Darwin survives!

Darwin is the root -- indeed the taproot that unleashed utter destruction upon humanity by justifying and institutionalizing racism and White Supremacy, race genocide, eugenics, rampaging atheism, and sexism/misogyny. Darwin's scientific and anthropological *bona fides* provided cover for all those who followed. Marx's works continue because the foundations of his work are Darwinist. This means unless Darwin's theories are "canceled," the scourge of grotesque outcomes will continue to rampage around the globe under the label of Marxism, Cultural Marxism and "wokeism."

The facts supplied in the preceding pages about Marx and his fervent reliance on Darwinism should raise many questions. Those who are awakening and are not knee-jerk ideological, but rather are wise, prudent and thoughtful, will begin to ask questions similar to the following:

- *How can businesses, corporations, and organizations who kowtow to woke mobs assert they are ethical while standing with those who encourage race superiority (Darwinist White Supremacy) and scientific racism (eugenics and Planned Parenthood) embodied in Cultural Marxism? Should business ethics include rejecting hateful and destructive doctrines and movements?*

- *Now that historical precedents have been uncovered connecting Marx/Marxism to Darwin's racism, White Supremacy, genocide, the active and intentional undermining of existing social order (including nuclear family, business and economies, and faith/religion), how should we respond to Marxism as it influences our schools/curriculum (K- college)? How should we respond to school boards as they thoroughly embrace all Darwinian theories and significantly pivot toward the diabolical reprobation of Marxism and Critical Theories?*

- *Since Marx used Darwin's terms referring to Blacks as gorillas (and worse), when will we demand a public renouncement and denouncement of Marx? Knowing how Marx and Engels felt about Blacks and other ethnic minorities, aren't those who continue to support Marx/Marxism/Cultural Marxism (and associated accouterments) by definition "racist," "White Supremacist," "eugenicists"?*

- *Marx was a confirmed racist, white supremacist, womanizer, enslaver, pathetic and ungroomed moocher, virulently God-hating, non-working grifter! Why is he respected at all? Why would anyone associate or align with Karl Marx? Hasn't Marx earned the right to be loathed and rejected by all?*

- *After considering their history and backgrounds, then reflecting on the respective influence they had on the worst despots in the history of mankind, can you name any redeeming factors in support of Darwin or Karl Marx?*

While coming out of slavery in the 1800's, educator, author, orator Booker T Washington overcame extreme violence and oppression. His experiences led to the profound understanding that confirms just because "the masses" (majority) are mindlessly pursuing agendas with great momentum, it doesn't make it "right." Wokeism is the perfect example of Mr. Washington's' assertion! His exact comment is as follows: ***"A lie doesn't become truth, wrong doesn't become right, and evil doesn't become good, just because it's accepted by a majority." ~ Booker T. Washington***

Getting WOKEd Up!?

Chapter Six
God Damns Darwinism!

He that believeth and is baptized shall be saved; <u>but he that believeth not shall be damned.</u>

~ *Mark 16:16*

With the background and expertise as a "Naturalist," Darwin worked diligently and theorized about how the earth and mankind came into existence. However, he relied solely on what can be perceived and naturally created in the material world; this is what precipitated his unleashing of "the theory of evolution." Darwin's evolutionary theory wholly relies on the premises that there is no God, no Creator, and no basis for humans (and the earth) other than as a result of evolution. In short, evolutionary theory is wholly atheistic, as it denies any semblance of a creator or designer God.

Darwin's "world-changing" influence was not limited to racism and White Supremacy. Atheism (similarly) existed before Darwin's declaration about evolution, but by adding his ontological and scientific declarations, many viewed atheism as having received scientific justification. Atheist materialism – the worldview that reality is comprised of only physical matter and energy, with no transcendent being to create, maintain, or intervene in it --was subsequently accepted and institutionalized based on Darwin's naturalist declaration of evolution. As the famous biologist Richard Dawkins proclaimed: "Darwin made it possible to be an intellectually fulfilled atheist."[42] Darwin's unleashing of his evolutionary theories injected atheism into the public square with great acceleration and increased cultural acceptance.

Atheism is foundational to Darwinian theories. It was popularized, scientifically "justified," culturally embraced, and unleashed as absolute confirmation that there is no God/Creator. Historical facts confirm: Social Darwinism, Marxism (including cultural Marxism), socialism, communism, eugenics are all rooted in Darwinism, and Darwinism is firmly rooted in atheism. Trouble is: In God's eyes, anyone or anything that undermines His divine authority is damnable. This means all adherents, disciples, or fervent followers of theories/philosophies directly undermining and subverting God's authority (e.g., Darwinism, Marxism, etc.) are also damnable.

No doubt many will contemplate the severe eternal consequences of following Darwin, or the many adherents of Darwin coming after him and attempt to excuse or exempt themselves by saying their acceptance of Darwinian views is tangential to their core beliefs. Trying to dance around Darwinism fails, however, because the ultimate test is: "What is Darwin's fruit?"

Compromising with Darwinian ideas will pollute a person's overall worldview and give evil results. Matthew 7:15-18 reminds us, "Beware of false prophets, which come to you in sheep's clothing, but inwardly they are ravening wolves. Ye shall know them by their fruits. Do men gather grapes of thorns, or figs of thistles? Even so every good tree bringeth forth good fruit; but a corrupt tree bringeth forth evil fruit. A good tree cannot bring forth evil fruit, neither can a corrupt tree bring forth good fruit." This means that if the "root" is evil, then the fruit is always evil – *it has to be*. It is impossible for a tainted root to produce good fruit. The inconvenient truth is, that there is no amount of gaslighting or equivocation that can get one out of the trap of Darwinism.

Suppose you adhere to any of Darwin's theories or works (or those of his followers, like Marx, etc.). You will unequivocally be tethered to their evil "fruit." The only way out is to reject Darwin and all his works (including racism, white supremacy, genocide, eugenics, and atheism). Rejecting Darwin should be easy after realizing his most fervent followers are marauding irreligious killers, virulently hateful of God.

In his book, *Reflections on a Ravaged Century* (1999) and *The Great Terror* (1990), author Robert Conquest wrote of Darwinism-based Marxism and Nazism:

Organized irreligion in the twentieth century committed atrocities on a scale that the fiercest religious wars never approached. The scientific racism of Nazi Germany killed forty million and attempted genocide against Europe's Jews. The scientific socialism of the Communist countries killed a hundred million (and still counting) people around the globe.

Darwinian disciple: Vladimir Lenin

Hate for God is another fundamental characteristic of Darwin's followers. Vladimir Lenin attributed his mind frame to Darwin. Lenin also was fervently atheistic and stated in his essay, "Socialism and Religion" (1905):

Our propaganda necessarily includes the propaganda of atheism ...We shall now probably have to follow the advice Engels once gave to the German Socialists: to translate and widely disseminate the literature of the eighteenth-century French Enlighteners and atheists.

Lenin was a Darwinist and a strong proponent and adherent of Karl Marx. Of Marx, he stated, "religion is the opium of the people – this dictum by Marx is the cornerstone of the whole Marxist outlook on religion." In 1909, Lenin wrote on behalf of "Social Democrats," stating, "It *is the absolute duty of Social-democrats to make a public statement of their attitude towards religion." Social-Democracy basses its whole world outlook on scientific socialism, i.e., Marxism. As Marx and Engels repeatedly declared, the philosophical basis of Marxism is dialectical materialism -- materialism which is absolutely atheistic and positively hostile to all religions.* Lenin made it clear: "We must combat religion- that is the ABC of all materialism and consequently of Marxism."[43]*

As Lenin was rooted in Darwinism, he was compelled by intrinsic evil and wholly captivated by Marx. Marx has many followers that persistently proliferate to this day. It is no secret Karl Marx and Marxism are primary drivers for modern-day atheistic narratives. Considering his gross and pathetic personal life, why is he so revered?

Karl Marx: A fervently zealous Darwinian disciple

Few people seem to know Karl Marx lived a grossly pathetic existence. He was known to be constantly agitated and angry, perpetually aggrieved, hateful toward those who dissented from his maniacal ideologies, and resentful toward those who would not tolerate his tirades. His persona was so horribly notorious that when he died, only about 12 people attended his funeral. Yet, even though Marx was a miscreant of the highest order, ironically, he continues to have a profound effect on the world as a supposed champion of everyday people.

We can imagine the reason why Marx is still heralded among elitists and in intellectual circles, is because most people have not connected the dots with Marx-inspired socialist and communist revolutions that have led to rampant racism, mass murders, enslavement, torture, and starvation of tens of millions of people around the world. Historians have estimated that in the attempt to make that "new" and "better" socialist world, communist regimes have killed as many as 200 million people in the twentieth century. Additionally, people laud and herald Marx because they fail to connect his respective roots to Darwinism and atheism (fundamentally interconnected).

Marx's hubris and insatiable hate encouraged him to advocate an ideology that supports genocide, mass murder, and dictatorships in place of the establishment of liberal democracies. Moreover, with his embrace of virulent atheism (reinforced by Darwin), Marx and his followers were emboldened to unleash grotesque immoralities and suffering without any guilt or perceived consequence. Ultimately, Marx embedded his personal embrace of anti-God demonism, grievance, and bitterness and integrated these soul-destroying elements into his political philosophy (communism). His philosophy overlayed mass movements and cultures within societies to propel radical Marxist revolutionaries around the world.

There are three fundamental underpinnings of Marx's ideology: (1) elitism; (2) specific- group superiority, racism, and eugenics; and (3) atheism (with his most pronounced motivation being a zeal to dethrone God). While most would assert economic philosophy was Marx's primary drive and "sweet-spot," Marx mainly was committed to hating God; he really didn't care whether this came from his economic philosophy or through cultural influences. That said, he viewed the economic underpinnings of Marxism as secondary; his virulent anti-God atheism was first. Marx notoriously stated, "Communism abolishes eternal truths." He declared openly in *The Communist Manifesto* (1848), "It abolishes all religion, and all morality, instead of constituting them on a new basis." He went on to declare,

"Communism begins where atheism begins!" This means that Marxism upholds a wholly atheistic and (therefore demonic) infrastructure based on a continuum starting with socialism as the first step, then to Marxism, then to communism; these stages of Marxist ideology are fundamentally designed to undermine and "dethrone God."

Today, Marx's legacy and diabolical deeds are being propelled via works led by a motivated army of Marxist "revolutionaries." The growth of Marxism has been substantial and continuous. With the extension of neo-Marxist revolutionaries aggressively agitating under the current parlance of "wokeism," Marxism has accelerated, not slowed. Nevertheless, we cannot ignore the obvious truth: Under the auspices of "woke," Marxism is a cultural force to be reckoned with. The evil scourge unleashed by Darwinist theories, then foundationally incorporated within Marxist theories, continues with renewed vigor.

As evil rampages, we must remember: These are the exact results Marx sought. He was not passive but quite zealously attacked all existing systems undergirding civil societies. This is especially true of his attacks on religion. Of Christianity, Marx stated: *"The social principles of Christianity preach cowardice, self-contempt, abasement, submission, humility. The social principles of Christianity are hypocritical.... So much for the social principles of Christianity."*[44]

While Marx abusively dismissed any notion of God, he was quite obsessed (smitten) with the Devil. He wrote poems and plays about characters making pacts with Satan and are therefore resigned to their own damnation. He even told his children bedtime stories with demonic/devilish themes. (Of note, Marx had two daughters and their respective husbands who died in suicide pacts. They were also atheistic revolutionaries like their father.)

In his work, *The Gulag Archipelago*, Alexander Solzhenitsyn states, *"Within the philosophical system of Marx... hatred of God is the principal driving force."* There's no escaping the fact that the hate for God and religion is ubiquitous within Marxist philosophy. Both Marx and Engels stated that *in order to achieve "the success of the cause ... it is necessary that man himself should suffer a massive change." This change must come through "a revolution," a process of "overthrowing" the old "filthy yoke." His "generation," like the Jews whom Moses led out of the wilderness, must "conquer a new world" and "must also perish in order to make room for the people who are fit for a new world."*[45]

To get to the desired utopia, Marx and his inspired revolutionaries had to take down the Judeo-Christian foundation: not just Christianity, but Judaism also. "The Israelite faith is repulsive to me," said Marx. It's quite telling that in his essay declaring religion "the opium of the people," Marx said that "the criticism of religion is the beginning of all criticism."

Marx's communist philosophy has brought forth an embrace of virulent atheism, and this has prompted profound actions and disastrous societal outcomes delivered by his communist followers. Over at least a century now, many have tried Marxism (including socialism/Marxism/communism). Still, not one culture or society has implemented any aspect of Marx's revolutionary utopia that has successfully helped citizens succeed. Instead, mass death, severe economic chaos, and utter destruction have always ensued. All of these examples confirm that you cannot receive good *fruit* (outcomes) from a rotten *tree*. The analogous Marxist *"tree"* is indeed diseased and rotten to the *roots*.

Marx's *root* of aggressive hate for religion has led to numerous instances of religious individuals and clergy being horribly maligned and killed in keeping with communist fervor and dictates. Pastor Richard Wurmbrand provides a stark example of communist- led Christian torture. Pastor Wurmbrand endured over a decade in a Marx-inspired communist prison just because he was a Christian and wouldn't renounce his Faith. Pastor Wurmbrand detailed unspeakable cruelty witnessed and personally endured in a Romanian prison in his book, *Tortured for Christ* (1967). His experiences are filled with unimaginable horrors.

Pastor Wurmbrand confirms that, because of their faith, Christians living in and around Romania were rounded up (men, women, and even children) and imprisoned; they were forced to endure gratuitous torture. With demonic glee, security guards would starve, beat, and torture with red-hot iron pokers and knives. The communists raged as they mocked Christ while forcing imprisoned clergymen to "consecrate" the excrement from other prisoners (and mixed with urine), and then give "Holy Communion" to Christian prisoners in this form. Marx's utopian dreams of worldwide communism carry an obvious downside (including dehumanizing torture and death) for Christians.

In the book *The Devil's Mill* and *The Hell of Pitesti*, additional accounts of Christian torture are characterized as a demonic torture chamber.[46] It conveys that because Christian "inmates" would not renounce their Faith, communist guards would force some prisoners to be baptized each morning by having their heads plunged into a bucket of urine and fecal matter (collected from other prisoners) while other prisoners chanted the ritual of baptism. This grotesque torture would last until the contents of the bucket started to bubble (with the person almost drowning in it). Then, the prisoner would be given a short time to catch his breath, then resubmerged.

It is hard to imagine the permanent and incalculable damage to the soul these forms of torture left on those who had to endure it. Please understand, due to the guards' (Marx-inspired) virulently evil hate for "religion," Christians were forced to drink urine and eat feces as prominent forms of dehumanization and torture! In communistic societies, gratuitous torture of Christians was not an anomaly, it was pervasive. From a Marxist standpoint, torturous activities directed at Christians were necessary to assuredly, as he put it, "dethrone God."

In addition to other documented evils, Marx was an extreme fatalist. He had a favorite quote from Goethe's Faust: "Everything that exists deserves to perish." In a letter to Arnold Ruge, he called for the "ruthless criticism of all that exists." The ruthless criticism that Marx and Engels most eagerly dispensed was targeted at religions; they felt their attacks would ultimately precipitate the church's demise and hasten their welcome to hell. In one of his poems, "The Pale Maiden" (1837), Marx fatalistically declared, "Thus heaven I forfeited, I know it full well. My soul once true to God, is chosen for hell." His hellish convictions help explain why Marxist revolutionaries are known for their relentless attacks on "faith" (generally). As you sit shaking your head in disbelief, ask yourself, "Has *anything* good, wholesome, honest and true come by way of Karl Marx (or his respective ideology)?"

In his book *Civilization* (2011), author Niall Ferguson mentions the words of a CASS (Chinese Academy of Social Sciences) scholar, *"We have realized that the heart of your culture is your religion: Christianity. That is why the West has been so powerful. The Christian moral foundation of social and cultural life was what made possible the emergence of capitalism and then the successful transition to democratic politics.*" The Chinese have rightly concluded that the Bible is anti-Marxist and anti-statist; therefore, to destroy America from within, the infiltration of the church was essential. Since Darwin "scientifically justified" it, the unleashing of atheism via Marxism produced aggressive and unrelenting attacks on church. Some churches recognize the existential threat Marxism poses to the soul, but regrettably far too many do not.

Marxist attacks on the Church

The Roman Catholic Church early-on understood the anti-God philosophies of Marx. It condemned communism as a "satanic scourge" conceived by "the sons of darkness." Of socialism, in 1931 Pope Pius XI issued his seminal Quadragesimo Anno, where he stated: "Religious socialism, Christian socialism, are contradictory terms; no one can be at the same time a good Catholic and a true socialist." This observation was accurate but not universally appreciated. Through strategy and tactics deployed by Marxist revolutionaries, many churches (and religions) ultimately accommodated and succumbed to Marxism over time.

In 1907, the Methodist Federation for Social Action ignored the obvious antithetical foundations of Marx and (under the auspices of Christendom) embraced Marxism. The purpose of this Federation was to redirect the church's focus to the suffering of the working class. The organization supported labor unions, tarred capitalism as "unchristian," and advocated an economic system based on central planning. It also spoke for the erasure of privilege and discrimination based on class or group identity. Many organizations and "clergy" have supported Marxism; most persist to this day.

There seem to be countless Marxist revolutionaries operating within and outside of the church. While there are far too many to highlight, one especially influential Marxist subversive deserves mention due to his numerous works: Dr. Joseph Fletcher. Fletcher graduated from the Berkeley Divinity School and was a self-proclaimed "democratic socialist" who taught at the Episcopal Divinity School, Cambridge, MA, and the Harvard Divinity School from the mid-1940s to the seventies. His work in the church centered on social justice and workers' rights. Fletcher helped establish Planned Parenthood, the Soviet-American Friendship Society, and the Society for the Right to Die. He became a leader in the field of bioethics, which he used to justify abortion and euthanasia. In 1966, contrary to church doctrine and teachings, he wrote *Situation Ethics,* advancing the idea that "there is no fixed morality, morality depends on the situation or circumstances" – a justification for abandoning the Bible. He was one of the most influential pastors in the U.S. and actively supported the Communist Party USA (CPUSA) – the main Soviet front of the day. He transformed the church to accept the idea that ethics are flexible and eventually abandoned Christianity for atheism.[47] Dr. Fletcher was a Marxist revolutionary who brought current levels of antithetical debasement and abject demonism to be more widely acceptable within the Church. The result: There are far too many churches participating with and readily imbibing Marx- inspired demonic delusions.

Vile hatred, persecution, and delusions about dethroning God via actively degrading and undermining "Faith" are Marx's hallmark and (regrettable) achievement. With an army of Marxist revolutionaries, Marx's evil legacy thrives within the church. Today's Marxist revolutionary forces are most apparent with woke Progressive Clergy. These people rely on "Social Justice," Liberation theology/Black

Liberation Theology and Critical Race Theory (CRT) as primary aspects of their messaging. Make no mistake, these theologies are not only unbiblical, but since they are wholly Marxist, they are also wholly demonic. If you happen to be under the leadership of a woke pastor (or minister), *run!* If you intend to reject the embrace of Marx's demonic evils that undermine spiritual formation and produce an existential threat to your very soul, *run!* Alas, basic Darwinism gave "scientific" cover for these cultural features today.[48]

As we see with his devotee Marx, Darwin's impact on humankind's view of God and religion cannot be overstated. Despite opposing voices, we must resist the urge to pretend Darwin's influence on anti-God momentum, and atheistic progression over the past century is negligible or benign. There is no sugarcoating Darwin or his theories. His influence on the Naturalist viewpoint and subsequent societal chaos resulting from scientific generation and justification of atheism is clear. Disciples of Darwinist ideologies (like Marx and Engels) have ushered in prolonged periods of utter destruction, death, mayhem, and the active undermining of major swaths of human existence within all societies and cultures worldwide.

Both Darwin and Marx deserve serious consideration; that's why this book exists. While contemplating all that has been uncovered about them, some will undoubtedly be tempted to "split hairs" because of a desire to continue embracing certain aspects of their theories (without fully embracing the attendant atheistic evils). Let me help. There is no splitting hairs!

The entirety of Darwin and Marx must be rejected. Recall: Matthew 7:15 says, "every good tree bringeth forth good fruit; but a corrupt tree bringeth forth evil fruit." This means only good trees can bring forth good *fruit*. So, the question is simple, "Did Darwinian roots start a *good tree* with good/healthy *roots*?" If you're sincere in answering this question, you would consider the generations of carnage, death and destruction precipitated by Darwin and definitively answer *no!* Therefore, there cannot be any semblance of good fruit to be leveraged from Darwin or Marx. They must both be rejected.

Today, wokesters (wittingly or unwittingly) carry the revolutionary mantle that Marx declared necessary. The clarion moment is immediate; it is now. The now-known facts confirm rampant evils and demonism, so will those who self-identify as woke continue their embrace of Marx's manifest evils? If so, can they be considered a great example of those Lenin deemed "useful idiots?" At the end of the day, will they continue the embrace – or will they wholly reject and denounce – all ideologies that most prominently proliferate anti-God, mass-murdering, eugenics-fostering, elitist-fomenting, racism and White Supremacy movements?

Some questions worth contemplating about Darwin's atheism and Marx's evils are:

- *Major movements, Darwinism, social Darwinism, Marxism, cultural Marxism, and now wokeism are born of the same taproot of atheism. If you're not an atheist, explain how you would you justify following and comporting to the ideological dictates of these maniacal atheists?*

- *Marx's primary goal was/is to dethrone God. His revolutionaries are compelled to carry forth this mission. If you embrace any aspect of Marxism, do you consider yourself an atheistic revolutionary?*

- *Good "fruit" cannot come from a bad tree with rotten "roots." Suppose you embrace aspects of Darwinism and/or Marxism, but are a person of Faith. Does that make you what Lenin characterized as a "useful idiot" (a person who confirms to an ideology's demands regardless of his or her personal ethics or commitment)?*

- *How do you respond to Marx's manifest evils if you're woke (self- described), and now recognize "wokeism's" connection to revolutionary Marxism and the manifest death, racism, supremacy/elitism, social destruction, mayhem, and virulent atheism (which undermines Gods moral authority and sovereignty)? Are you principled or merely ideologically (non-thinking and uncompassionate) driven to continue as a Marxist revolutionary?*

- *Two fundamental yet pervasive elements wholly contrary to America's founding are racism and atheism. Both are interwoven within Darwinism and cultural Marxism. That said, do you see why Marx embraced, relied on, and unleashed these elements (via revolutionaries) to subvert the established order in America?*

- *Recognizing the truth of Jesus's advisory that you cannot get good fruit from a rotten tree, can clergy support aspects of Marxism (with atheism baked-in), and still remain faithful to the Gospel? Can businesses remain faithful to corporate ethics (to create value for shareholders), while also embracing woke Marxist policies (or social movements)? Can individuals who purport to be "anti-racists" sincerely support the roots (and fruits) of Darwin's scientific racism and the grotesque social impact of Marx/Marxism (including eugenics, genocide, race classifications, etc.)?*

- *There are (regrettably) many neo-"religious" theologies. Some are foundationally based in Marxism (like Liberation Theology and Black Liberation*

Theology). Isn't it impossible for sincere "people of Faith" to now ignore the inconvenient truths of Karl Marx, his hatefully virulent atheism, the history of communist torment of Christians, and myriad demonic evils that been unleashed due to Marxism? Can persons of Faith continue to embrace Marxism while also in honest pursuit of God and his Kingdom?

- *Are there any ways to accommodate both Marxism and sincere "Faith"? Based on Marx's hatred of God and his proclaimed desire to "dethrone him," can these ideologies coexist even though they are toxically diametric and have opposites and objectives on "polar extremes"?*

Karl Marx demanded a total disregard and abandonment of God. The totality of his works and theories are wholly committed to his goal of "dethroning God." That said, all those who follow Marx, Marxism, and his predecessor Darwin or Darwinism, are following a course with a curse and are damned! As a reminder, *"He that believeth and is baptized shall be saved; but he that believeth not shall be damned." ~ Mark 16:16 (Holy Bible)*

There is still much to awaken to. Are you "WOKEd Up" yet?

CHAPTER SEVEN

DARWIN'S MISSIONAL MISOGYNY

BRAZENLY PIONEERING THE "WAR ON WOMEN!"

"Knowledge will forever govern ignorance: And people who mean to be their own governors must arm themselves with the power knowledge gives"

~ James Madison

Sexism and misogyny are ancient evils; they have repeatedly occurred since the beginning of man. Suppose these scourges against women were purposely unleashed with "scientific justification" and given modern-day vigor out of malicious intent. Should the person who unleashed them be forever held with disdain and contempt? Hold that thought.

Ticking off a litany of Darwinian evils can become tedious and mundane. Ugh! Racism, White Supremacy, genocide, eugenics, and atheism all constitute significant human activity and affect human well-being domains. And Darwin permanently (negatively) impacted them all.

Darwin's impact on the whole of humanity is so (regrettably) pervasive that we must ask, "Are there any domains that remain free from the roots of Darwin's evil influences?" Since women widely esteem him, we would think this is undoubtedly a domain free from any subversive influences from Darwin, right? Wrong! Through intensive study and a series of experiments, Darwin unleashed additional linguistic distinctions that undermine

94

women/womanhood as well. Considering the facts, *Darwin was actually an early general in "the war on women!"* Darwin popularized and escalated sexism and misogyny through his works and associated theories. On top of all the other evils he fomented, it's hard to think, but it's true: Darwin weaponized his scientific justifications to pave the way for entrenched sexism and misogyny.

Darwin was a scientist and Naturalist. Naturalists rely heavily on natural, observable phenomena to make assessments. To this end, Darwin made assertions about cranial size in order to confirm observations and assessments about brain size and respective intellectual function. Fundamentally, he wanted to arrive at a scientific rationale for determining intellect; these experiments were conducted to help distinguish between races and biological genders. Regrettably, Darwin's theories along these lines were flawed and produced conclusions about women that only much later were determined to be far off-base. Taken at face value, however, his findings gave rise to sexism and misogyny. Acceleration of the abuse and defamation of women was a natural byproduct of his theories.

Michael Flannery summarizes Darwin's profound "sexism" as follows:

Darwin's views on gender were equally benighted. In *Descent of Man*, Darwin referred to men's superior "inventive genius" over women because of their "absolutely larger" brains. He continued, "The chief distinction in the intellectual powers of the two sexes is shown by man's attaining to a higher eminence, in whatever he takes up than can woman - whether requiring deep thought, reason, or imagination, or merely the use of the senses and hands. If two lists were made of the most eminent men and women in poetry, painting, sculpture, music (inclusive both of composition and performance), history, science, and philosophy, with half a dozen names under each subject, the two lists would not bear comparison."[49]

Of course, Darwin never considered that men dominated these fields, and within Victorian patriarchal society, most women would have been precluded from entry in the first place. Darwin's list merely reflects prevailing cultural prejudices, not inherent science-based capacities.

Sigh. Darwin again used the power and authority of his "scientific" proclamations to conveniently prop up superiority themes that buttress "patriarchy" while undermining humanity. This time the target of Darwin's unscientific theories and conclusions was women.

In his book *The Decent of Man*, Darwin asserts, "We may also infer, from the law of the deviation of averages, so well illustrated by Mr. Galton in his work on 'Hereditary Genius,' that if men are capable of decided eminence over women in many subjects, the average standard of mental power in man must be above that of women." Darwin's words bespoke his belief in in male dominance and preeminence over women. He was chauvinistic, sexist, and misogynistic. Notably, the unleashing of Darwin's delusional theory solidified the supremacy of the patriarchy while justifying subjugation, unequal treatment, and abuse of women. Based on Darwin's "scientific" assessments, he cemented himself as a principal instigator of "the war on women."

As documented in my 2020 book, *The War on Women from the Root to The Fruit: Which side are you on?*, women are the foundation for nurturing all of humanity. All humans are born/birthed via women, and God made this is an inescapable reality. As part of Darwin's revolt against god, it is no surprise elitist patriarchal machinations from Darwin would inevitably target women.

After Darwin's releasing *The Descent of Man* in the late 1800s, women found themselves fighting all the more for "equal rights as men," voting rights, and against a scourge of domestic violence. Women innately knew they were equals and possessed God-ordained privileges to birth and nurture humanity. Still, they were summarily thwarted and undermined by accelerated cultural trends of male chauvinism and brazen misogyny. Emerging trends toward contempt for any notions that women should be viewed as equal to men prompted the start of the "women's suffrage" movement.

Darwin's insidious impact on women's suffrage

The war on women prompted by Darwin made women fight for equal rights during the "women's suffrage" movement. Women had to combat in a war unleashed by Darwin's purported scientific confirmation and explanation of their supposed intellectual deficiencies. With evident hostilities, hatred, and notable enemies (including laws and precedents) targeted at women, women's suffrage was seen and internalized as an actual battle and war.

One example that demonstrates how women internalized their fight and plight in the battle for women appears in the popular 1964 movie "Mary Poppins," where Mrs. Banks sang: "We're clearly soldiers in petticoats, And dauntless crusaders for woman's votes, Though we adore men individually, We agree that as a group they're rather stupid! Cast off the shackles of yesterday! Shoulder to shoulder into the fray! Our daughters' daughters will adore us and they'll sing in grateful chorus, 'Well done, Sister Suffragette!'" No thanks to Darwin or his disciples, the suffrage movement gained great support worldwide, creating a push to amend the U.S. Constitution.

The women's suffrage movement was significant for combatting the Darwin-sponsored cultural tide's onslaught toward dominance of White male "patriarchy." (Note: This is the exact nomenclature wokesters invoke today while wholly supporting Darwinism! But, I digress...). A prominent leader in the suffrage movement was Susan B. Anthony. Susan B. Anthony had an earnest desire to see women simply become equal in stature and influence to men. She worked tirelessly to help illuminate the rigors and woes of all women, and in doing so, she also became a beacon of light and hope for Black women who were raped, abused, and treated as mere "property" as a result of being enslaved. There were many Black women maligned and abused due to slavery, which led to the abolitionist/civil rights movement and the women's suffrage movements to align closely. Frederick Douglass and Susan B Anthony became friends and colleagues as it became ever more apparent that abolitionist goals and women's suffrage goals aligned as primary human rights goals.

The importance of the immense works and successes in changing the trajectory for women cannot be overstated. Darwin unleashed a societal trend to target and undermine women, while Susan B. Anthony tirelessly worked to combat sexist evils that disparaged and disempowered women. Susan B. Anthony has been dutifully heralded as a pioneer and American heroine for all.

The suffrage movement gained prominence and momentum during the same period Darwin unleashed his book, "The Descent of Man, and Selection in Relation to Sex," portraying women as unequal and deficient. This movement was indeed important and necessary, as, before the efforts of Susan B. Anthony, Frederick Douglass, and Elizabeth Cady Stanton, women were being treated horribly and abused without restraint. The collaborative efforts of this team necessarily raised issues for equal rights, human sensibilities, and new laws that would then protect women.

Karl Marx's aspersions upon women

As a Darwin disciple, Karl Marx also had disparaging feelings about women. This is not surprising since Marx insisted on upending all existing traditions and cornerstones of humanity. Since women have a significant role in birthing humanity, they are principally a God-ordained cornerstone for humankind. As a sniveling and pathetic anti-God miscreant, Marx likely felt no compunction or guilt about not paying and then using his live-in maid as a sex slave. Based on his actions, Marx obviously felt justified in the maligning and subjugation of women.

To be sure, Marx was outspokenly candid about his preference for males. In letters, Marx lamented to Engels that "My wife, alas, delivered a girl, not a boy" (he regretted to Engels of his wife's birthing abilities). When his daughter gave birth to a baby girl, Marx wearily commented, "I congratulate you...I prefer the 'male' sex..." Marx again provides clear confirmation of the degree to which he was a wholly dedicated and strident disciple of Darwin. There is no better example of "toxic masculinity" (and the abuse therein), than Darwin and Marx. An inconvenient and undeniable fact is that Darwin and Marx held malignant contempt for women.

A major aspect of wokeism rejects "toxic masculinity" and "the patriarchy"; wokesters purportedly fight against the "war on women" by standing on behalf of women who are maltreated, abused or disparaged. Wokesters now have another data point, however, confirming the need to reject and denounce Darwinism and Marxism (and all associated accouterments). With what's been uncovered about

Darwin's pioneering works and theories that led to the initiation of a "war on women," and Marx's kindred spirit with Darwin in this regard, all women should reject these men and their respective ideologies. In addition to all other noted domains, these men and their followers failed horribly when it came to fair and equal consideration and treatment of women as well. If we're sincere and consistent, shouldn't both Darwin and Marx be "canceled?"

It's a fair question: Why haven't Darwin and his devotee Marx been canceled? How is it their respective support among women grows while their anti-woman ideologies persist as they assault all womankind?

There is an insidious "blinding effect" that takes place when the pull of seductive and compelling (albeit arcanely wicked) ideology is coupled with dominant cultural forces demanding meek compliance. People we would otherwise deem as thoughtful and intelligent become pathetically weak, cowardly, impotent, and sheepish caricatures of the principled resoluteness every American should share. Are "wokesters" mere "revolutionary tools" being used to enforce demands of evil yet pervasive cultural forces?

That depends. If wokesters continue zeal for Marxism even after discovering all that has now been factually documented about Darwinist's racism, supremacy & sexism combined with Marxism's embrace of the same coupled with the push for an atheistic global revolution, then, yes, they are mere tools. Such tools are what Lenin described as "useful idiots" (a term Lenin used not for disrespect but to describe a simple fact).

For those who are not lazy or too intimidated to think deeper about the weighty issues that have been uncovered, many questions should be asked and considered at this point. Some of those questions are:

- *With Darwin and Marx's subsequent derision of women, can anyone sincerely stand for women and against sexism, while also fully embracing Marxist-inspired wokeism? Unless both Darwin and Marx are denounced, the internal contradiction presents a challenge: is wokeism a form of principled activism, or does it lack principles so that wokesters are driven by duplicity and hypocrisy? They can't have it both ways and expect to be taken seriously. They either publicly denounce the Darwin-Marx ideology or prove they're wholly unserious.*

- *Can wokeism be taken seriously if its followers continue to willfully ignore and deliberately overlook the foundational roots of sexism and misogyny as "scientifically justified" and popularized by Darwin and Marx?*

- *Can the entire sphere of modern-day feminists/feminism be taken seriously if feminists fail to reject Darwin and Marx? Shouldn't feminists who rant about canceling a past U.S. president about purportedly "sexist" tweets be expected to at least appear to be consistent by also immediately demanding cancellation of Darwin and Marx?*

- *Following the truism that we cannot receive "good fruit" fruit from a "rotten tree," can any political entity, education entity (or professor), corporation (or business), agency or organization sincerely assert a commitment to supporting and embracing "women" while also fully supporting and endorsing sexism and misogyny of Darwin and Marx (that is baked into the woke ideology)?*

An **honest social activist cannot sensibly embrace anti-women people and ideas while simultaneously claiming to be pro-women.** Therefore, to be consistent with wokeism's sound bite activism, all entities must immediately publicly denounce and renounce Darwin and Marx (and their respective ideologies), or they are tacitly confirming their participation in rampant "useful idiocy!"

Many women fall in line with woke ideology without full knowledge of the sexist mindsets governing Darwinism and Marxism, the roots of wokeism. For over a century, these mindsets dominated and subjected and set women back. Founding Father James Madison provides great encouragement for those with the courage to grasp the depth of knowledge (albeit inconvenient) now offered: ***"Knowledge will forever govern ignorance: And people who mean to be their own governors must arm themselves with the power knowledge gives"*** ~ *James Madison*

WOKEd Up? Awakened? Angry? Stay alert!

CHAPTER EIGHT

MASTERFULLY MANIACAL MANIPULATORS!

"Political language is designed to make lies sound truthful and murder respectable."

~ George Orwell

"Master class" level manipulators are responsible for the rapid scale and adoption of "wokeism." For any social movement to gain significant and unwavering social acceptance, it must be led by people who are masterful in articulating objectives and visions that resonate with the masses. To garner a considerable following of groups wholly embracing and stridently following nebulous and insidious social movements (like wokeism, for instance) requires those who are genuinely masterful maniacal manipulators—master-class manipulators who have influenced and perpetuated wokeism need to be exposed and stopped.

This book aims to deliver a society-wide "wake-up" call. As you read, you'll see emerge a clear pattern of masterful manipulators. Those manipulators are experts at using false narratives to motivate action. For example, Darwin used false scientific narratives to motivate others to embrace a new way of viewing "creation" and the human condition. His theories enabled Marx (and other megalomaniacal figures) to deploy scientific justifications as means to begin permanently changing the order of things within civil societies.

Following masterful manipulators and embracing their schemes have led to boundless mass horrors and atrocities.

Motivated minions carrying forward Darwin and Marx's racism, supremacy, eugenics, atheism, and sexism are not driven by principles of truth and love, they're unfortunately blinded by the zeal of disgusting false narratives. This book strives to eradicate this affliction. Make no mistake, while "wokesters" are the revolutionaries for afflicting culture with false narratives, most of them can be awakened with *truth*.

It's high time for mass awakening! Master manipulators have been celebrated and esteemed, but the historical facts reveal the truth that drives away the darkness while awakening hearts and minds. In the battle to combat racism, supremacy, and the myriad cultural ills, "wokesters" must awaken. The time is now.

Most all societies have been asleep while grossly vile people have manipulated the masses to spread diabolical evils around the globe. That's not a surprise, really. It is common for people to be taken for granted or used as unknowing pawns to help wickedly motivated but mostly invisible hands achieve diabolical ends. Few decent people would eagerly self-identify as a wokester if their sincere efforts, intentions, and motivations are misdirected or nullified because of unscrupulous hypocrisy. Becoming a tool of manipulators just makes them look like a joke, not woke! The thought would be appalling that their sincere efforts are misrepresented, and that theyare used and abused through manipulations. This book has been carefully researched and written with these thoughts in mind.

Lenin scoffed as he celebrated the works of "useful idiots," and this book is written to declare Lenin's era of manipulating "useful idiots" is over. Now is the time for sincere people with sincere motivations to finally do what is right. We are now transitioning to a resolution that will end the "rotten fruits" born of a wicked tree and root system.

Now is the time we finally lay an ax to the taproot of racism and White Supremacy in America. Now is the time we metaphorically chop down the evil tree from its fully exposed wicked "taproot."

This book has documented many evil individuals, demonic global despots, and wicked social activist provocateurs (like Margret Sanger) who took the mantle of racism and White Supremacy and aggressively expanded it through false narratives and strategic manipulations. After Darwin used his influence and authority to underwrite and unleash racism by recklessly utilizing his theories as "scientific justification," its acceleration has been (regrettably) tremendous. And over a billion innocent people have lost their lives because of it (including the impact of eugenics/abortion).

It is past time we take inventory of the body count that Darwin amassed globally due to his nefarious theories. Again, while evils have existed since the beginning of man, consider that most evils were "opportunistic" and not the product of deep fundamental groundwork. This fact kept the evils relatively constrained (to certain regions or eras). It wasn't until Darwin utilized his scientific studies and his craven mind to unleash new linguistic distinctions and theories that gave anthropological credence to:

- Racism
- White Supremacy
- Genocide
- Eugenics
- Atheism
- Sexism and misogyny

We have witnessed ideas presented as logical, factual, or reasonable grounds to take action in society; only the evilest and demented hearts among us glom onto them and attempt to use them as levers of manipulation. People caught in the thrall of these ideas then justify the use of these agenda-driven distinctions to terrorize others. Ultimately, the vilest persons embodying the vilest personalities aggressively use Darwin's scientific justifications (for racism, genocide, eugenics, sexism, etc.) to pursue personal agendas without restraint. If any barriers or dissenting voices emerge while despotic personalities pursue their personal agendas, they will receive the full brunt of unfettered and aggressive Darwin-inspired actions. As a disciple of Darwin, Marx is the perfect example of unhinged contemptuous evil that can be unleashed.

Marx's impact on today's wokesters

As noted, Marx was perpetually aggrieved, agitated, and insatiably motivated by hate. In his peculiar mind, utopia is achieved only after God is "dethroned" (all peoples become atheists), and there is a period of constant chaos and conflict between "the masses." He wanted every system (thought of as the prevailing hegemony) to be undermined and overturned. Marxist ideas thus inspire wokesters to attack all hegemonic forces and overturn them.

Marx's disciples started divisive and racist Critical Race Theory (CRT), followed by cultural agitation using "Critical Social Justice" to bring America to the point where we can observe Marx's dreams of total transformation via complete upheaval in America becoming quite plausible. Today, wokesters invested heart and soul serving as fundamental vectors carrying forward Marx's dream of revolution. It's way past time for an actual awakening (or, better yet, reawakening) within the ranks of self-described wokesters in America.

Let's cast off the malaise and get "WOKEd Up" because we repeatedly have been purposely manipulated. We see how Darwin manipulated science. His disciples and adherents (turned despots) manipulated "the masses." And Marx carried Darwin's "scientific justifications" forward to massively manipulate political philosophy and "religion." The Marxist goal of undermining humanity means the tactic of manipulation is always in play. The primary tool activists use to create mass movements in culture is *manipulating gullible people*. They always look to recruit people who are well-intended but, in their personal zeal, will blindly follow an ideology. Blindly following ideology is what allows individuals to become "useful idiots."

Useful idiots are now being relied upon to help establish a global cabal committed to another "utopian" goal: a global "great reset." This effort relies on a global network of agitated "wokesters" to create untenable chaos throughout societies and cultures worldwide. Guilting, shaming, doxxing, castigating and terrorizing dissenters are all now commonplace. To masterful manipulators, these actions are necessary, strategic, and purposeful.

The wokesters live in a nightmare of an unprecedented level of deception

Wokesters are being heavily marketed to and encouraged to embrace self-deception. Even in serious "scientific" and "scholarly" works, wokesters demand people reject logic, reason, prudence, and even mathematics and science, in order to advance their transformative mission. Wokesters are driven to willingly allow themselves to be emotionally manipulated to the extent that both the racist science of Darwin and Marx's abusive political philosophies energize the push toward a one-world government utopia. If someone asks, "What does a wokester's embrace of Darwin's racist/supremacist science and of Marx's political philosophies look like in today's world?" The answer is everywhere in divisive, hate- and resentment-filled, anti-logical, socially- destructive, and infanticidal rhetoric receiving praise in academia, politics, and the media.

If wokesters could be truly awakened, the trajectory of moral decadence and societal degradation would immediately change to the positive. But, alas, Darwinist and Marxist influences persist. An example of wokesters' embrace of Darwin appears in the rampant escalation of eugenics-based laws and policies, infanticide (sex-selected abortions and murder of newly born), and a growing cadre of global elitists declaring that ending the life of the unborn is now somehow viewed as "enlightened" and should be celebrated. Even U.S. lawmakers are now attempting to permanently codify new laws guaranteeing abortion (on demand) up to the time of birth.

In the same vein, wokesters' willful embrace of Marx's abusive political philosophies are obvious as they (such as BLM) proudly declare their Marxist allegiance despite knowing his philosophies (socialism/Marxism/communism) have failed wherever implemented. The effects of manipulation cause wokesters to willfully disregard horrible atrocities and millions of lost lives due to Marx's communism. They also pretend complete ignorance about the fact that Marx himself was a racist and sexist "pig!" Wokesters rely on the emotional momentum that carries the movement while wholly ignoring their personal ideological blindness. The wokeism phenomenon conclusively proves ideological blindness exists, and maniacal manipulation persists!

Wokesters: the ultimate Marxist revolutionaries

Wokesters fit Marx's dream of unleashing global revolutionaries perfectly. As noted, Marx's goals viewed everything with a critical lens with a plan to destroy everything as it currently exists (all business/institutions, including marriage/family, religion, education, media, and entertainment). The blind ideological allegiance of wokesters is essential for upending things as Marx wanted. Constantly agitating and resolving to remain perpetually aggrieved while lacking any capacity for forgiveness – that is the world of wokeness.

Remember, Marxism needed and therefore demanded coercion, despotism, and outright terror from its inception. Marx called for all three. In his essay, "The Victory of the Counter-Revolution in Vienna," Marx wrote, "There is only one way in which the murderous death agonies of the old society and the bloody birth throes of the new society can be shortened, simplified and concentrated, and that way is revolutionary terror." Can Marx's agenda be any clearer? Marx's own words explain why Marxist wokesters are agitated, constantly encouraging caustic chaos, and seeking to overthrow all "hegemonic" paradigms that currently exist.

Modern-Day Marxism

For many, Marxism is somewhat nuanced and harder to detect in America. However, most modern-day diehard Marxists can be recognized easier under the auspices of Saul Alinsky. Saul Alinsky was a notorious community organizer in the 1960s and 70's; his modern-day Marxist tactics are foremost in the playbook of today's woke movement.

Using Karl Marx's playbook, Saul Alinsky provided a strategic blueprint for social activism in a book called Rules for Radicals (1971). Alinsky was a notable social malcontent and devious miscreant, as his writings consistently encouraged and embraced Karl Marx's socialist/communist agenda.

An overwhelming majority of Marxist community organizers likely use Alinsky's playbook; he garners a huge following that persists to this very day. Moreover, even after acknowledging and dedicating his works to Lucifer in the front pages of his book, he's been lauded by Presidents and Heads of State (B. Obama and H. Clinton are self- professed Alinsky disciples1213)![50, 51] So while Alinsky was a self-professed demoniac, some of the most influential people on the planet follow his blueprint as a virtual "bible" for building movements and changing culture. To be sure, Alinsky's dedication page reads as follows:

Lest we forget at least an over-the-shoulder acknowledgment to the very first radical: from all our legends, mythology and history (and who is to know where mythology leaves off and history begins--or which is which), the first radical known to man who rebelled against the establishment and did it so effectively that he at least won his own kingdom- Lucifer.[52]

It's clear Alinsky had dark motives and allegiances with dark forces in the demonic realm, yet again, his legacy is heralded and persists.

In his book "How Evil Works," author David Kupelian wrote Obama proclaimed, "Alinsky's community organizing rules were seared into my brain." Kupelian chronicles Alinsky's work as "the general public must be made to feel intimidated, upset, frustrated, and hopeless. Alinsky explains: Any revolutionary change must be preceded by a passive, affirmative, non-challenging attitude toward change among the mass of our people. They must feel so frustrated, so defeated, so lost, so fruitless in *the prevailing system that they are willing to let go of the past and change the future. This acceptance is the reformation essential to any revolution* (emphasis added).[53]

Other notable Saul Alinsky quotes from his book, "Rules for Radicals" are: "The first step in community organization is community disorganization. The disruption of the present organization is the first step ...The organizer must first rub raw the resentments of the people of the community; fan the latent hostilities of many of the people to the point of overt expression ...Search out controversy and issues, rather than avoid them, for unless there is controversy people are not concerned enough to act ...The organizer's first job is to create the issues or problems ...An organizer must stir up dissatisfaction and discontent ... The organizer ... polarizes the issue ...The organizer helps to lead his forces into conflict ... The real arena is corrupt and bloody... In war the end justifies almost any means."

There is no doubt Alinsky is one of the most influential masterful maniacal manipulators of our time. Alinsky's synopsis perfectly underscores how his diabolically inspired strategies are used to undermine existing mindsets and alter worldviews. Since his tactics are entirely designed to precipitate agitation, resentments, and an undue emphasis on "struggle," moral values and common sense should dictate his works must be wholly rejected. Still, alas, he's cheered as a "Progressive" champion. In addition to Alinsky dedicating his book to Lucifer, his entire Marxist methodology is designed to foment the base emotions of conflict and resentment to proffer hatred.

Alinsky asserts, "People cannot be free unless they are willing to sacrifice some of their interests to guarantee the freedom of others. The price of democracy is the ongoing pursuit of the common good by all of the people." That said, here is a list of Alinsky's 13 "Rules for Radicals":

1. "Power is not only what you have, but what the enemy thinks you have." Power is derived from 2 main sources – money and people. "Have-Nots" must build power from flesh and blood.

2. "Never go outside the expertise of your people." It results in confusion, fear and retreat. Feeling secure adds to the backbone of anyone.

3. "Whenever possible, go outside the expertise of the enemy." Look for ways to increase insecurity, anxiety and uncertainty.

4. "Make the enemy live up to its own book of rules." If the rule is that every letter gets a reply, send 30,000 letters. You can kill them with this because no one can possibly obey all of their own rules.

5. "Ridicule is man's most potent weapon." There is no defense. It's irrational. It's infuriating. It also works as a key pressure point to force the enemy into concessions.

6. "A good tactic is one your people enjoy." They'll keep doing it without urging and come back to do more. They're doing their thing, and will even suggest better ones.

7. "A tactic that drags on too long becomes a drag." Don't become old news.

8. "Keep the pressure on. Never let up." Keep trying new things to keep the opposition off balance. As the opposition masters one approach, hit them from the flank with something new.

9. "The threat is usually more terrifying than the thing itself." Imagination and ego can dream up many more consequences than any activist.

10. "The major premise for tactics is the development of operations that will maintain a constant pressure upon the opposition." It is this unceasing pressure that results in the reactions from the opposition that are essential for the success of the campaign.

11. "If you push a negative hard enough, it will push through and become a positive." Violence from the other side can win the public to your side because the public sympathizes with the underdog.

12. "The price of a successful attack is a constructive alternative." Never let the enemy score points because you're caught without a solution to the problem.

13. "Pick the target, freeze it, personalize it, and polarize it." Cut off the support network and isolate the target from sympathy. Go after people and not institutions; people hurt faster than institutions.

It is likely, that we can personally identify with several of these Alinsky "rules" (or tactics). The importance of these rules in the context of wokeism is, wokesters will (wittingly or unwittingly) use these tactics. They are designed to provide a secure place for wokesters to maintain an "upper hand" in discussions and activism.

When open and collaborative discussions devolve into emotions boiling over, wokesters launch into ridicule, guilting, and shaming. This is classic Marx/Alinsky! Insult about someone's thoughts and opinions by demanding they be disregarded due to their relative lack of education is quite common. When you see this tactic, recognize it as one of Alinsky's standard "rules."

As Alinskyite agitators (masquerading as today's wokesters) attempt to manipulate to change mindsets and worldviews, they'll only succeed if (as Alinsky asserts) "they (the masses) are willing to let go of the past and change the future. This acceptance is the reformation essential to any revolution." This confirms that if those who reject wokeism hold fast to our logic, prudence, and Biblical traditions, we gain the capacity to deny joining diabolical Marxist social movements and forestall strategic attacks on a personal worldview that undermines our cherished traditions. Today, however, our culture and society are not too thoughtful and wise, so we must pray.

Like his predecessor Marx, Alinsky was a sad and pathetic demoniac. His followers and self-professed disciples are the wokesters of today, and regrettably, they are also miserable and pathetic. We must recognize classic Alinsky symptoms as they persist within the woke movement and show mercy to people trapped in this pitiful mindset. They need much sincere prayer to break the stronghold of demonic oppression.

Awakening wokesters

Recall again the Biblical text declaring, "you will know the truth, and the truth will make you free" guides the process of becoming awakened. You can feel truly free when you come to grips with the many inconvenient facts, truths, and sinister deeds of those who have historically been lauded and esteemed. Ideally, fair-minded persons who are self-proclaimed wokesters reading this book will experience an epiphany that uplifts them with the strength to escape from being used by evil forces.

We want all to be awakened by the voices of truth. When the truth is known, the people who stubbornly hold onto the ideologies of racist/supremacist Charles Darwin and follower Karl Marx with his racist/sexist, global terrorist machinations, would deserve universal disdain. It is unjust for us to further the divisions. The weak-minded and disgustingly pathetic deserve compassion, of course. To prevent even more division and hate, we must learn to tolerate the pitiful and demoralized. To tolerate does not mean to agree or accept deceptions and evils. But from a Christian perspective, Marx- embracing wokesters need prayer, not in-kind hate.

Wokesters who will remain undeterred in their embrace and fervency for the emotional manipulation of Marxists are (regrettably) pathetically demoralized. Demoralization is typically the issue when we see people stubbornly committed to reprobation. Merriam Webster's dictionary defines the word "demoralize" as "to cause to turn aside or away from what is good or true or morally right: to corrupt the morals of." Also, "to weaken the morale of." Lastly, "to upset or destroy the normal functioning of."

The reason why German citizens who saw the trains full and heard the screams of Jews (during Hitler's genocidal terror) yet did nothing about it is a perfect example of mass demoralization. Marxist/communist guards who tortured Christians in prisons went to extremes to maim, kill, and demoralize them in the most inhumane ways (to the point of having them eat feces and drink the urine of other prisoners) did so because the guards themselves were demoralized. The blind emotionalism of wokeism is similar.

The reason why wokesters recognize racist/supremacist deeds yet still hold steadfast to Darwinism, Marxism, and the eugenics of Margret Sanger's Planned Parenthood is that they are perpetually aggrieved and wholly demoralized. Normal logical thought processes are disrupted and suppressed, while emotionalism-dominated ideological demoralizations become the commanding drivers to produce actions and deeds. Realizing pitiful, pathetic, and easily manipulated "wokesters" are driven solely by ideology, we recognize they are currently "unreachable" and desperately need the help and support of prayer. Breaking free from enshrined ideology is nearly impossible without prayer intervention. Being ensnared in the woke ideology makes the life of wokesters torturous, not sublime.

Breaking free

Have you ever wondered why every time you encounter a wokester, they seem to be angry and agitated? Fundamentally, it's because wokesters live a life filled with arcane duplicity brought on by the need to embrace narratives they know deep-down are false. Remember, embracing the truth sets one free. But wokesters are forced to willingly deceive themselves, then try to become comfortable with living a life of brazen hypocrisy and self-deception. This approach layers on and exacerbates agitation and aggrievement. Anger and hate are obvious by-products of wokesters recognizing their condition of being trapped in a veritable cocoon of deception. Deception both "justifies" them in their rhetoric while it condemns them in their conscience.

Wokesters noisily castigate capitalism while lauding and venerating the communism of Marx (even though his political theories have never helped but also hurt the "poor" and "marginalized"). Does it make sense to hate the system (capitalism) that's pulled more people out of poverty, while ignoring Marxism's furits of death and destruction? The woke (at times) claim they rely on science. Yet, when science confirms human life begins at conception, they demand babies in the womb are merely a "clump of cells" that could/should be "exterminated" (a Sanger characterization). How can anyone demand reliance on science while simultaneously rejecting science (especially when it is inconvenient)? While wokesters demand the end to "America's systemic racism," they hold fast to the actual systemic racism (modern-day eugenics) of Planned Parenthood as it targets Blacks for "extermination" How can any person or institution that is sincerely "anti-racist" and anti-White Supremacist support strategically targeted racist murder of Blacks via "abortuaries?"

While they advocate for unfettered Marxism and eliminating "the rich," they fully embrace capitalist lifestyles by purchasing multiple homes (BLM founders and Bernie Sanders are great examples of this), as well as buying expensive cars?

One especially pitiful example occurred when a recent woke judge nominated to the U.S. Supreme Court stated she couldn't define what "a woman" is and was applauded and confirmed for being "enlightened" (Progressives claim to feel defining "women" somehow undermines and insults "trans" people). Yet, when the U.S. Supreme Court in 2022 overturned the *Roe v. Wade* decision that had declared abortion a federal constitutional right, the same Progressives were hysterically screaming about abortion as being essential for "women," having no qualms about using the term when it comes to supporting the killing of babies)! The utter foundational contradiction stares us in the face: "Are there still 'women,' or aren't there?"

These few examples out of many illustrate the hypocrisy and duplicity that wokesters must reconcile internally. Such a condition of mind is called cognitive dissonance, which prompts people to resort to woefully deceiving themselves in arcane ideological mental gymnastics.

Rabid revolutionaries

One of the most apropos descriptors of the woke movement (and wokesters generally), is "rabid." Merriam Webster's dictionary defines the term rabid as, "raging;

uncontrollable." "Extremely zealous or enthusiastic; fanatical." It also confirms rabid as, "of or affected by rabies." These descriptors are "on point," as all of these definitions apply to wokesters. (Except maybe the affliction by biological rabies.)

Many Americans can easily attest to being yelled at and castigated if they utter even the slightest dissent from woke/Progressive talking points. This behavior meets the exact definition of rabid when coupled with extreme zeal and seemingly uncontrollable rage wokesters embrace for their ideological ends. Because of their uncontrollable zeal, the revealed facts describing the historical diabolical roots of their revolutionary movement will not likely dissuade rabid wokesters. In their minds, the fervent embrace of wokeism is unbreakable, and their movement, unimpeachable. This is why some view (as I do) that the pathetic wokeism movement deserves our pity.

When viewing pictures or hearing of animals that suffer with rabies, our normal reaction is to feel pity for them. We recognize that when stricken with the rabies virus, animals lose normal brain function; anxiety, confusion, and agitation becomes their torment. This is exactly what happens to rabid wokesters. They imbibe a "virus" that consumes them and clouds their thinking and discernment. They seemingly lose "normal" brain function pertaining to logic, reason, and "common-sense." They agitate and lash-out as they (sometimes) turn hostile and violent. Notably, agitation becomes wokesters' torment as well, because actions and logic-patterns are altered. Individuals lost in the grips of insanity (as we view rabid animals) is a painful, pitiful sight.

Fraudulently feuding

This book shows how any individual or institution that pretends to be awakened and enlightened while venerating Darwin or Darwinism is a fraud. Any individual or institution that asserts being awakened and culturally astute while venerating and embracing Darwin's follower, Marx (or any of his theories), is likewise a fraud. Any individual or institution (including businesses, education, entertainment or political entities) who "beats their chest," socially preening about their stand against racism while embracing any aspect of racist eugenicist, Margaret Sanger or Planned Parenthood, is a fraud.

Here's the nub of the matter. If we presume there is pervasive "systemic racism" in America and that it's the most significant problem in America, then we must universally denounce and renounce the roots of it. This means we must denounce and renounce Charles Darwin and Karl Marx. We must finally "cancel" them and their respective racist, supremacist, genocidal, atheistic, sexist theories. We must no longer tolerate trying to have it both ways. We must awaken and no longer tolerate living life as duplicitous frauds.

The embrace of Marx/Marxism is an example of wokesters' trying to have it both ways. Most wokesters don't ascribe to or condone Marx's racism (including his gratuitous use of the "n" word to describe Blacks), sex-slavery of his live-in maid (she was poor, and worked tirelessly, yet he didn't pay her a cent), Marx's atheism and virulent hate for God, Marx's embrace of White Supremacy and eugenics as the driving force behind his genocidal machinations (via communism), or Marx's sexism (subjugating and undermining women). Yet, wokesters unthinkingly and unconditionally embrace Marx/Marxism. Why? Indeed: why on Earth?

The wokesters want it both ways. They want to be able to virtue signal by taking a public stand against racism and White Supremacy while never renouncing the roots and deeds of racist and White Supremacists. Let's face it, the essence and embodiment of racism and White Supremacy (past and present) is rooted in and runs deep with those who embrace Marxism (therefore Darwinism); the facts are inescapable. Anyone who embraces Marxism cannot escape the overflow of diabolical ideological concepts being funneled into their thinking (conscious and subconscious). Conscious purposeful renouncement of Marx and associated works and ideologies can begin the process of expunging the root of Darwin's taint on humanity.

Using an analogy to today's "cancel culture" helps clarify why denouncement of Marx/Marxism is not optional. Today, if someone befriends and is ideologically aligned with a well-known member of the KKK, that person is (reasonably) deemed a racist; and they are then "canceled." If someone is a friend and supporter of a racist, they are deemed to be also racist and "canceled." If someone doesn't support a KKK member but supports aspects of KKK ideology, they are deemed racist; they are "canceled."

The point is: *If we're sincere and consistent, this same process of "cancellation" must apply to Darwin/Darwinists and Marx/Marxists.* Following definitions and facts, all who align and embrace the racist ideologies of Darwin and Marx are racists and should be "canceled." Likewise, wokesters unendingly ranting about racism while carrying out the utopian dreams of Marx must be, for consistency's sake, "canceled."

Many of the problems we currently face in American society are not the result of the "systemic racism" of White male patriarchy. Many systemic problems stem from having conveniently ignored the historical roots of evil racist

120

machinations (and have allowed them to fester) to the point that we are divided, distrustful, hateful, and antagonistic toward one another. To remedy racist issues requires we no longer ignore the facts about those who scientifically justified (Darwin) and popularized philosophical movements (Marx) via lies and deceptions underlying and encouraging racism and other similar "isms."

Suppose sincere efforts are faithfully committed to confronting and combatting racism where it exists. In that case, we can begin to turn the tide. A pivot that changes the trajectory of racism in America is possible, but it can only be accomplished with non- ideological serious people wholly committed to standing on truth.

As documented throughout this book, the evil scourge of racism and White Supremacy became rampant. Along with the resulting banner of "justifications," grotesque genocide, race/sex inspired eugenics, terroristic atheism, and misogyny/sexism were also unleashed. As with the analogy of what happened when my dog Sparkle was unleashed, community havoc resulted. The only way to get control and stop further carnage is to restrain and re-tether. This is exactly what must be done with Darwin and his despicable theories and with Marx and his hideously insidious philosophies.

We cannot pick good fruit from a rotten tree, so going forward, anything connected to or relying on Marxist theory must be rejected. That includes rejecting "anti-racist" training that stems from the inbred tenets of Marxism. Likewise, since Critical Race Theory is founded and buttressed based on Marxism, it must also be disqualified. This means the violence and terroristic actions perpetrated by the Marxist/fascists who identify as "Antifa" must be rejected and denounced. It is impossible to combat racism in

America while (at the same time) aligning with the same racist theories, doctrines, and ideology that causes it.

Wokester solutions

There is a dire need for pure (non-ideological) education and training designed to expose the nefarious history of racism and White Supremacy and meaningfully erase it wherever it exists today. There is a dire need to activate and mobilize individuals and organizations determined to erase racism without erasing history (especially inconvenient history). There is a dire need to help pathetic and demoralized individuals by providing education and training to help them break free. Regrettably, existing "Anti-Racism" training based on Ibram X. Kendi's "How to be an Anti-Racist" are ineffective and impotent in dealing with the various (and in some cases pervasive) racist ideologies today.

Ibram X. Kendi's "Anti-Racism" training is not the answer for helping unite communities and providing aspirational alignment with truth. People who have taken those types of training and associated curricula report the training classes are designed to undermine American history and unmoor the Declaration and U.S. Constitution from their foundations and founders (under the guise of "upending" the "Patriarchy"), by "gaslighting" about history. Such training/educational sessions seem to only create more animus and distrust in the end. Likewise, gratuitous agitation and insidious false narratives are embraced, leaving many participants feeling like the training aims to "totally transform America" (including history, traditions, and laws) through cultural forces that project mechanisms of guilt, shame and "cancellation."

Fundamentally, "Anti-Racism" training imbibes nefarious influences of social Darwinism and Marxism; these are influences subtly embraced and unleashed towrd finally bringing forth the diabolical utopian objectives of a God-less, soulless, mindlessly gullible ideological transformation that undermines civil societies (just as Marx dreamed). We understand now: It is impossible for anything that relies on fruit from the evil Darwinian tree to bring forth good fruit like unity and peace among races, "classes," genders, and myriad workforces. So, if this specific type of training ("Anti-Racist") is not the answer, then what is the answer that will help us unify and trust one another again?

Answer: personal training that focuses on *truth* and is designed to help ease race conflict, ideological blindness, and demoralization. Irrespective of how some people virtue signal and socially preen about being involved with "Anti-Racism" training, the evils of racism cannot be banished with these types of ideologically woke methods. I have no doubt these types of training give some participants "warm-fuzzies," but that doesn't actually help ease divisiveness and hate being experienced throughout society. Much of these "anti-racism" training programs are purposely grievance-focused, consciousness-raising, struggle sessions. In the end, many participants don't feel they are more empowered to deal with race issues, they don't feel unified. Social science research and anecdotal reports both reveal that participants experience *increased levels of divisiveness and distrust* after this training.

If the advertised promises of sincere healing and forgiveness are not the actual expected outcomes (take-aways) from Anti-Racist training, then true social unity and more racially-sensitive communities cannot be produced. We must not forget that many people – individuals - are sincerely hurt and need healing. Therefore, healing and forgiveness are fundamental - and individuals must receive both for them to progress to racial harmony.

Addressing racism and supremacy in America starts with a determined look at root causes. As confirmed throughout this book, the roots are false narratives precipitated by Darwinist theories; these "roots and fruits" must be fully exposed and addressed. From there, it is easier to begin to connect the dots in history to uncover where society and cultures began to pivot in the wrong direction. After correcting the lies and deceptions perpetrated by major scientific and cultural icons of Darwin and then Marx, appropriate narratives confirming the truth about their schemes and deeds can come forth. *Exposing the truth is the key.*

The Razism Strategy

Truth is always obscured if it is ignored and largely hidden because of ideology. Nothing should be "sacred" or off-limits when to comes to conveying truth. Healing and unity can begin to come forth when we let the truth be "truth" – and deceptive lies "be damned!" With truth, we can and must work to demolish racism. To coin a phrase: We need a commitment to get racism "razed!"

Throughout this book, we factually confirmed the roots and structures of racism and White Supremacy. We have seen the interconntect circle: Marx – Darwin – racism – interest-group warfare – eugenics – group-based hate and distrust – agitation – chaos – blaming and condemning whole groups and populations – "training" to cement permanent group divisions and distrust. It is high time to demolish the intellectual roots of racism and group distrust.

Razing occurs when entire structures are thoroughly demolished. Darwin and Marx's racist structures need to be razed. And that's the aim of the new "Razed" education/training by Every Black Life Matters (EBLM). Razed training and education are designed to expose racism's root and structures as a way to demolish them. We are committed to raising a righteous revolutionary force of "hell razers" (a cadre of trained individuals committed to identify and demolish racism and supremacy wherever it occurs) to combat the revolutionary forces of Marxist hell-raisers!

Existing "racial reconciliation" and "anti-racism" training efforts fail to produce healing and unity because they leave the racist roots and structures untouched and in place.

In contrast to prevailing anti-racism education and training, razism training builds unity and commitment by helping all (especially the ideologically demoralized) to see and confront historical truths via exposing facts that undo the damage of sociopaths of the past. It starts by clarifying the divine significance of every life by confirming that God has a divine plan for everyone. His plan portends equality, irrespective of race/ethnicity, gender, or other classifications, without partiality. With that in mind, razism training is designed to identify and actively demolish racism wherever it exists without ideological equivocation. Fundamentally, razism uniquely brings forth the good fruits of humanity because it stems from the incorruptible roots of "the truth." Anyone can and should become a committed razist advocate.

With a unique emphasis on racist structures, razist training is much more effective for producing interpersonal change and intervention than other purported "anti-racism" alternatives. Those who become even minimally competent in understanding the distinctions of razism will become razist advocates. The primary unique characteristic of advocates is their holistic rejection of *all* racism in *all* domains at *all* times (even if "inconvenient"). This is the only way to accelerate the capacity to observe and then begin to seriously address the multi-complex issue of racism. One of the most important characteristics of razism: It is not political and not at all about appeasing prevailing cultural ideology; it's strictly about confronting the "roots" and structures of racism and ending it.

Once qualified, a razist advocate will never again conveniently partner or coddle an ideological position rooted in racism (like Darwinism, "Social Justice," Marxism, or the beliefs and programs of any particular political party) because it helps drive an ideological or political outcome; razist advocates will fully understand this is wholly unprincipled and "unserious!" Razism is to be taken seriously because it is utterly committed to advancing the principled voice of truth.

The prevailing cultural tide of wokeism desperately needs to transition over to real principles for helping eradicate racism via razism. This is the only way we will be able to take prior wokesters seriously. Non-ideological and sincere wokesters should immediately get certified to be razist Advocates (see www.everyblm.com for info) so bridges can begin to be built and our broken culture/society can move forward.

Wokesters who are sincere about rejecting their current state of being ideologically demoralized, and who desire to become awakened, enlightened, and hold others accountable for doing the same, must commit to becoming razist advocates. Razism education and training can fully prepare individuals to defend against and give account for prior support of Darwinism, Marxism, and resulting actions from the entirety of the worst racist, genocidal, sexist despots in humankind's history. Notably, this requires some level of contrition, repentance, and forgiveness, so this is not an easy step for typical narcissistic and prideful wokesters.

Woksters may be horribly misguided and ideologically blinded, but their state is not permanent. Nevertheless, those who so desire can be reconciled and unified. The critical step of embracing razism is necessary, however. The razism process helps individuals truly commit to a new and more effective way to process the racist/supremacist pain of the past.

The Four Life-Changing Steps of "Four-giveness"

No one can move forward and progress in their life if they are perpetually aggrieved by (virtual) chains of false narratives of the past. In this condition, they are immobilized and inconsolable by ideas that agitate them to become hateful, distrustful, accusatory, and unable to walk the path God divinely created for them. Chains of false narratives can be broken by truth, repentance, and forgiveness. These are key elements that constitute the taproot of the "good tree" and therefore bring forth "good fruit." These are also the steps that must be taken to ensure a baseline that encourages sincere reconciliation and unity going forward. Tapping into the good fruits of razism follows a process that begins with exposing accurate historical truths as the starting point. Like light, truth is a disinfectant that eradicates wokeism evils by exposing lies, and this allows the breaking up of the fallow ground of a hardened soul. After the truth has defined a baseline, the process of reconciling and unifying one to another can begin. To that end, I have created a "Four-giveness" model for reconciliation. The "Four-giveness" model has four steps to take in order:

(1) Contrition/Brokenness: After the truth is exposed, we feel some level of contrition. That means feeling sorry, feeling remorseful for having followed a wrong path that

hurt ourselves or other people. We're not alone: we've all been exposed to grotesque lies proffered via culture at some point in our lives. Many of us have fully embraced and participated in those lies (i.e., Darwinism, Marxism, eugenics, sexism, etc.), and realizing this should bring brokenness and contrition.

(2) Repentance: After contrition comes repentance. Contrition means realizing we are fallible and can be unwittingly (and with best intentions) deceived. It also builds resolve for integrity so that we will work diligently to not allow ourselves to be deceived and used as a "pawn" going forward. That understanding leads to repentance. That's when we recognize what has happened in the past, expressing our regret for it, and personally committing to "changing direction" so as to not follow the wrong path and not repeat the harmful things we've said or done. Some public examples of entities that should repent in order to truly reconcile are:

(a) Woke school districts that embrace Darwinism and Marxism;

(b) Woke corporations who support Marxist organizations (like BLM and Antifa), and also support racist eugenics schemes of Planned Parenthood; and

(c) Woke sports teams that hysterically decry "White Supremacy," while fully supporting socialism (therefore Marxism) and the Marxism of BLM.

These examples are some of the most obvious (though many) due to their ideological hypocrisy.

(3) Forgiveness: While all steps in the razist learning process are designed to erase racism, *the most vital is forgiveness*. The Bible declares, "If you do not forgive, neither will your Father in heaven forgive you! (Mark 11:25-26). A heart that sincerely embraces forgiveness is

required to be set free and to become all we were created to be. Anger and bitterness rooted in CRT, "social justice," and Marxism, cannot increase when forgiveness is embraced. These antithetical movements would be restrained and rendered powerless with the simple act of forgiveness. Forgiveness is needed to help us individually reconcile with what happened in the past (be it former spouse or employer, historical hurts from slavery, or any number of unresolved issues). By embracing it, we heal and are able to move forward in life. Sadly, many people are so weak-minded and demoralized that they will continue to reject forgiveness and choose to remain complicit in allowing their soul to be cemented in the abyss of darkness. It's awful but true: Some people seem to prefer remaining in bondage to the evil of unforgiveness instead of being set free, thus blindly embracing negative ideology produces that result.

(4) Unity: The final step to achieving harmony and reconciliation – whether with people we know or between groups of people – is to experience unity! We can sincerely unify when the truth is exposed, contrition is acknowledged, and we actively repent and then extend forgiveness. We can only unify and reconcile when we don't hold grudges and bitterness toward others. Jesus' message, indeed the message of the Bible to all humankind, is to "love your neighbor," and that means discarding hate, anger, and resentment. Whether you're a Christian, Jew, or from another worldview, this message should ring true in your heart and mind.

Above all, the process of Four-giveness is rooted in the truth. But here's the challenge: Wokesters have now two different possible paths. Some will see Four-giveness as a way to break free from living in the bondage and duplicity of woke culture. Others will prefer living with no repentance, extending no forgiveness, and constantly demanding perpetual penance from others. These folks' pitiful souls hang in the balance and are in desperate need of prayer. While their devious manipulators have long passed away, their torments persist.

Questions wokesters must face

Many questions related to the gross machinations of masterful maniacal manipulators should be addressed. Some immediate questions include:

- *Because it is impossible to get "good fruit" from trees with rotten "roots," it is impossible to embrace Darwinism and yet assert rejection of racism, White Supremacy, atheism, eugenics, and sexism. So how can a curriculum in almost all education systems (K-college) embrace Darwin while socially preening about being woke and standing against racism?*

- *Similarly, why do the wokeism advocates fail to confront the grotesque hypocrisy of educational systems (teachers and professors), sports teams, corporations and business entities, the entertainment industry, politicians, BLM/Antifa, and countless other entities who actively embrace the covert forms of Marx/Marxism, while the wokeism advocates actively purport to stand against racism, supremacy, and sexism?*

- *Relatedly: Should ignorance about Marx's racist rants, his sex slavery of the family maid, his embrace of Darwin, his virulent hate for God, and his violent terroristic ideology that has led to hundreds of millions of deaths, be excused and ignored? Should any/all entities who embrace Marx be held accountable for the evil embrace of his brazen manipulative ideology?*

- *Realizing Ibram X. Kendi's "Anti-Racism" training is based in Marxism and actually teaches that prejudice and racist actions targeted against Whites is okay: How is it "Anti-Racist" at all?*

- *How can supposed Marxists remain interested in enriching themselves – which then do – when "the wealthy" are Marxism's primary targets?*

- *What excuses avowed socialists (i.e. Marxists) like Bernie Sanders, and Marxists in BLM when they act fully "capitalistic" when buying mansions?*

- *Additionally, Ibram X. Kendi and Robin DeAngelo (Marxists and CRT proponents) reportedly demand tens of thousands of dollars per hour when publicly speaking. Why do Marxists have any interest in attempts to maximize their personal fortunes if they're sincerely Marxists?*

Is it logical for education systems/schools to "cancel" historical books they deem racist and supremacist while vigorously embracing an educational curriculum that relies on diabolically racist/supremacist theories from the person (Darwin) who "scientifically justified" racism, atheism, sexism, eugenics, and mass genocide? Based on Marx's history and deeds (including racism, sexism, virulent atheism, and eugenics), can wokesters logically embrace Marx/Marxism as they virtue signal about being "woke?"

Is it logical and ethical for capitalist businesses to embrace Marxist organizations (like BLM and Antifa), knowing Marx was racist, sexist, racist, eugenicist, and genocidal? Shouldn't they be confronted about this duplicitous hypocrisy?

Shouldn't woke journalists and politicians who proclaim to stand against racism be held accountable for standing with Planned Parenthood's racist/eugenics? Shouldn't they be standing against Marxism in any form? Shouldn't they be held accountable for their reckless embrace of racist ideas popularized by deceptive manipulators?

Since there is alternative training to the woke "Anti-Racism" (Marxism-inspired) training that will help wokesters heal and unify, shouldn't wokesters now begin to embrace the truth, repentance, and forgiveness of Raze-ism?

For too long, we have allowed nuanced language to veil actual deeds. Woke, anti- racism, and the oblique embrace of Marxism are great examples of how wretched schemes can use language to obscure manifest evils. Novelist and journalist George Orwell said it best: ***"Political language is designed to make lies sound truthful and murder respectable"*** ~ ***George Orwell***

Y'all get WOKEd Up!

CHAPTER NINE
WOKESTERS OF THE WORLD AWAKEN

...GET WOKED UP!

"One of the most cowardly things ordinary people do is shut their eyes to facts"

~ C.S. Lewis

This book began by presenting the rhetorical question:

IF you could confirm modern-day racism, White Supremacy, genocide, eugenics, and sexism were propagated (and "scientifically" justified by one person, THEN would you hold that person in perpetual contempt and disdain? Would you 'cancel' that person?

Well, now is the time to answer the question!

This book aims to expose the fact that wokeism exists as a prevailing cultural theme; it is proliferating, and people who self-identify as being woke are suffering from a level of purposeful ideological blindness, and they genuinely need the intervention of truth. Truth is the disinfectant that breaks the chains of demoralization and malaise currently plaguing wokesters. *Truth can set them free!*

Wokesters need to be set free from delusional mindsets that survive and thrive by virtue signaling with vacuous screeds accusing, guilting, shaming, and "canceling" others while (at the same time) holding fast to an ideology that they purportedly protest and reject (i.e. racism and White Supremacy). Opened eyes can see wokeism in its current cultural context as duplicitous and hypocritical.

Unfortunately, hypocrisy is pervasive, but that doesn't mean we can continue to excuse it.

The death of democracy by deceptions

In 2017, the *Washington Post* adopted the slogan: "Democracy dies in darkness." The slogan rings true, but it was notably hypocritical for a newspaper that has itself been roundly accused of promoting Leftist/Progressive propaganda and, therefore is itself "anti-democratic." When a singular ideology (here, Leftism/Progressivism) is comingled with media, you get the perfect environment for launching mass movements motivated by ideology, not truth. In the end, democracy doesn't "die in darkness" – democracy undermined by deceptions dies "in the light of day!" Wokeism embodies the perfect example of this.

As wokeism becomes more and more hostile, intolerant, and violent against dissenting voices, we see the spirit of democracy dying every day, and its death is celebrated all along the way. Truth be told, wokesters are modern-day Marxist revolutionaries who assert democracy while wholly undermining democracy. Even the briefest reading of Soviet and Maoist history shows the cravenly deceptive use of words to conceal their opposites are true. George Orwell powerfully and unforgettably pointed out this fact in his legendary books, *1984* and *Animal Farm*. Wokesters are now emboldened to undermine and condemn the pillars of democracy (notably free speech, Second Amendment rights to self-defense, and the entire Bill of Rights), without even considering the disastrous outcomes such radical revolutions and subsequent outcomes these actions would invoke on a (fading) free society.

People who sincerely seek an end to racism and other hater idea systems must not automatically bow to the whims of woke media/propagandists and behind-the-scenes manipulators. Sincere wokesters should become eager to wonder: "Based on what has been exposed about Darwin's unleashing of modern-day racism and White Supremacy, are there any environments or circumstances where Darwin or Marx (and their respective ideologies) can be embraced or lauded?" Additionally, they should be inspired to ponder: "Can any sincere person who self-identifies as woke, embrace any aspect of Darwinism or Marxism going forward?" Lastly, they should consider: "Since recent 'mass shooters' involved in the Columbine High School massacre, Gilroy Garlic Festival (and others) are known to have been strident White nationalists motivated by strong Darwinian impulses, shouldn't we at least consider that Darwinian philosophies can be a key motivator for White supremacy, racism and mass shootings?

Regrettably, many will continue to fully embrace the racism, white supremacy, atheism, eugenics, and sexism of Darwin and Marx. The willingness to remain in thrall to evil ideas has been known for millennia and is captured in the New Testament at John 3:19- 20(ESV):

"And this is the judgment: the light has come into the world, and people loved the darkness rather than the light because their works were evil. For everyone who does wicked things hates the light and does not come to the light, lest his works should be exposed."

Without the triumph of truth, without a program like the Four-giveness, several very sad facts will endure:

- Those who are Nazi or KKK sympathizers that hate Jews and embrace the same anti-Semitism as did Marx, will continue to embrace his ideologies and laud him for them.

- Politicians and elitists who believe the old racist tropes that contend all Blacks who are born poor inevitably commit crimes, therefore Planned Parenthood is necessary to help "poor Blacks" self-eliminate, will continue to encourage and support the targeted racism and eugenics of Planned Parenthood.

Elitist teachers or professors who are delighted with Darwin's race/elitist classifications because those ideas elevate them to the top rung of "classes" in society will still stridently promote Darwin.

- Demoralized hostile and violent people who desire to restrict freedoms to bring about Marx's dream of "one-world government" (nowadays, the "Great Reset"), will continue gleefully supporting Marxist fascism (like that of cultural movements like BLM and Antifa); they'll fervently follow Marx straight to hell.

- Atheists who hold the same vitriolic hate for God as did Marx, will continue to love and embrace the ideologies of Darwin and Marx.

Clear knowledge presented in this book should persuade many people to pursue goodness and truth. Unfortunately, many others may still want to embrace evil as they languish in their self-deceptions. There are two clear paths demanding a clear and direct binary choice: Now is the time to choose!

The level of grotesque propaganda engulfing America over the past few years pretty much assures this book is likely to have a profound effect on some and only marginal to no impact on others. No change to their mindset will likely occur for those who are ideologically rigid and demoralized, and who are gullible to psychological projection from the media. Failing to accept the undeniable truths set forth in this book and the resources provided, such people tragically confirm they don't really care about the racism and toxic masculinity of Darwin and Marx. They only want optics and hysterics dictated by the Progressive (delusional) elites who have paved a specific path for weak- minded and pitifully pathetic individuals to continue their obedient goose-step. Only a divine intervention can help this motley crew.

The road to perdition is broad, neatly groomed, and paved with the souls of wokesters; those who persist in wokeism are destined for destruction therein. The purveyors of the path to perdition include modern-day neo-Marxists who, by definition, are complicit with racism and White Supremacism and are wholly supported by most public schools/boards, progressive clergy, politicians (both sides), media/news/anchors, woke corporations (e.g., Nike, Bank of America, Chase, Gerber, Disney, Apple, Amazon, Meta, Alphabet's Google) sports leagues/teams (MLB, NFL, NBA), globalist Marxist movements like World Economic Forum (WEF, BLM, Antifa) and education/training consultants embracing Critical Race Theory (CRT) and "Anti-Racism." Stripped of their rhetorical camouflage, the purveyors are all fundamentally those who advocate Progressive Leftist causes.

Simply stated: The hysterically shrill wokesters who rant about injustices of racism and White Supremacy are the same ones fully embracing the very ideologies that brought modern-day interpretations and deeds that uphold racism and white supremacy. Anyone sincere about addressing racism must publicly denounce and renounce both Darwin/Darwinist theories and Karl Marx and his Marxist followers.

After scrubbing off the traces of those killer ideologies, (former) wokesters can become Razism Advocates helping extinguish racism by exposing it and combatting it wherever it exists. Anything less confirms useful idiocy at best, or wholly complicit supremacy at worst.

Good news: This book proves all is not lost!

Pernicious wokeism presents our everyday challenge

True, Marxism's momentum and treacherous headwinds are significant, and the current trajectory of our wholly debased culture is clearly downward. But we can combat it by exposing the truth about Marx/Marxism, and, importantly, we can pray for Divine intervention. Both are critical ways we fight wokeism and begin to turn the tide.

Think about it: We're constantly harangued with statements and cultural hysterics that assert America's most pressing issues are systemic injustice due to systemic racism. Suppose racism is in fact "systemic" across America (as asserted). In that case, it is factually due to the systemically racist/supremacist themes and ideologies spread via educational curriculum fully endorsing Darwin/Darwinism. It is also due to the culture's' ubiquitous embrace and lauding of Marx. History confirms their diabolical ideologies and schemes to racially classify factions and (in the case of Marx) undermine civil society. Their culpability is inescapable!

Knowing the truth, going forward, it will be easy to confirm whether wokesters are sincere about addressing systemic racism or just remaining pathetically demoralized useful idiots (Lenin's appreciative characterization) happy to just participate as a Marxist "revolutionary" solely motivated by politics and social activism.

Five easy questions for everyday conversation

While this book especially spotlights wokeism as the fundamental issue for culture and societies globally, we can now see that wokeism is not the biggest socio/cultural problem. The main challenge we face globally is awakening wokesters, i.e., getting them "WOKEd Up!"

It's a big job, but it starts by asking the hard questions and requiring truthful answers from the wokesters and other decent people. Challenge these folks with this simple question:

Question 1: If a person, whether a scientist or anyone else, declared all Blacks are basically apes and savages, who you demand that person be immediately "canceled"?

The wokester must answer "yes," or that wokester isn't true to wokeism, right?

Question 2: If a scientific authority figure asserted (and "scientifically justified") that all whites are "superior" to every other race, would you immediately denounce and work diligently to "cancel" that supposed authority?

The wokester must answer "yes" again, or that wokester isn't true to wokeism, right?

Question 3: If a person or organization declared they are targeting all Blacks for extermination and that's ajustifiable and prudent policy, would you "cancel" them?

Here again, the wokester must answer "yes" or else contradict wokeism.

Question 4: If you learned someone is a loathsome grifter, womanizer and sex-slaver, you would report them to "authorities" and/or denounce and "cancel" them, right?

Any wokester, indeed any decent person, would have to answer "yes."

Question 5: If a public figure declared his or her abject hatred toward God, then went further to declare hate for Jews and Blacks, you'd immediately publicly denounce and work diligently "cancel" that hater, right?

Although some wokesters themselves hate God, they would still have to denounce and "cancel" the racist hater.

You will notice each of these challenges arises from our knowledge of Darwin, Marx, and their ideological followers. The facts are known, but, to this very day, the two malcontents and miscreants are lauded, applauded, and extolled, not canceled. There is no fair-minded, logical, humane reason why these people and their ideas get a free pass from CRT proponents and wokesters.

What we have learned

We learned earlier in this book:

- Darwin purposely chose to ignore and discount the first scientific anthropologist to classify races, Johann Friedrich Blumenbach, whose studies confirmed *no* scientific reason or rationale to classify Blacks as inferior to other races. Instead, Darwin unleashed the mindset that Blacks were inferior, deeming Blacks as apes/gorillas and savages. He was the first to provide "scientific justification" for modern-day racism and White Supremacy.

- Darwin and Galton specifically created eugenics (meaning "well-born") to provide justification for exterminating all ethnicities races (other than White (or "Aryan"). Ironically, that eugenics concept represents the fullness of White Supremacy and racism, but has been enshrined and embraced in all societies under the auspices of "women's rights."

- Planned Parenthood Founder Margret Sanger, an adherent of Darwinism, proudly declared she wanted to "exterminate Negros" and strategically located her "clinics" to meet this objective.

- Karl Marx was a loathsome, perpetually unemployed grifter who was a racist, a womanizer, and participated in the sex enslavement of his housekeeper. He also expressed virulent hate for God and called for upending all existing traditions and hegemony in deference to perpetual chaos and revolution.

Many other despots and cultural icons were mentioned in this book, but the point is clear. Based on what we know now if these loathsome individuals' respective works and ideologies should righteously be "canceled," then then these individuals should already be "canceled" by now.

We're more enlightened now, we're more conscious about injustices now, and were now….. WOKE'd UP!

There's a painful dilemma facing some readers. If you're one such reader, please understand the following challenges are offered to advance the cause of racial, indeed all human, harmony. So, please prayerfully consider:

Going forward, if you embrace Marx then, by definition, you *are racist*. It also means you believe in and practice race superiority and unforgiveness and are a Marxist "revolutionary." You cannot hide, because people with knowledge from this book can see you. You may assert being woke, but the truth unmasks you. Moreover, the essence and embodiment of racism and White Supremacy (past and present) is rooted in and runs deep with those who embrace Darwinism. Any person or entity embracing Darwin's works cannot escape the overflow of his

141

diabolical concepts being poured out into their thinking (conscious and subconscious).

Can you still embrace Darwinism with a straight face and a heart for racial harmony? Or can you instead consciously renounce Darwin and his works, and thereby help expunge Darwin's taint on humanity? Most especially should all school boards and educational institutions take this same action? Silence is not an option.

Dietrich Bonhoeffer, the martyred pastor, theologian, anti-Nazi dissident, proclaimed: "Silence in the face of evil is itself evil: God will not hold us guiltless. Not to speak is to speak. Not to act is to act." For those of us who have now been awakened and "WOKEd Up," silence is not an option. The answer to combatting modern-day racism and white supremacy is to attack its roots. That means rejecting Darwin and Marx. There is no other way. *Silence is not an option!*

Wokesters can't stand against racism while being complicit and silent about Darwin and Marx's racism. Everyone must make a binary decision and then take action. Very straightforward. Entities (individuals or organizations) can either stand with and for the demented "scientific justifications" that Darwin posited (and Marx and Sanger exploited), or they can work diligently to cancel those nefarious figures. Which side are you on? Which action will you take?

QUESTIONS AND ISSUES FOR REVIEW AND DISCUSSION

There are questions and data points that should come to mind. Some are:

- *"Do Black lives really matter?" If so, doesn't that mean you must take a stand against Planned Parenthood and its founder Margret Sanger? Doesn't that mean you must take an active stand against Darwinism and associated Marxism? Other than just talking about the significance of Black lives mattering, what public stand (and required denouncement) are you willing to do? What is your stance?*

- *Are you a true "anti-racist? If you embrace any Marxist teaching and training, you are not standing against racism, you support it. You are actually supporting what you supposedly want to fight against. By definition, Marxism actually defines you as a racist and supremacist. Anti-racism training that rejects Marxism is called "Razism" training. Will you become an Razism Advocate?*

- *We've heard some say, "only racists reject the tenets of CRT." But this is gaslighting. The truth is, only racists (by definition within CRT) are the ones who embrace CRT. This book shows CRT is founded in Marxism. Therefore, it is inescapably racist. It does not unite or help build trust, it does the opposite. Do you reject CRT? Does your school board reject CRT? Does your organization reject CRT?*

- *Now is the time for woke pastors/clergy and "Marxist" professors to reject this "America is systemically racist" notion. Unless they publicly denounce and renounce Marx, they are the racist ones exacerbating racism in America. Four- giveness is needed. What can you do to help clergy and professors see their folly, and renounce and repent?*

- *Ibram X. Kendi and Robin DeAngelo are Marxist-sympathizing authors who tout CRT and decry systemic racism as ubiquitous in every American domain. Based on Marx's actual racist history, shouldn't both Kendi and DeAngelo immediately disavow Marxism? If they don't, aren't they confirming they are demoralized and aggrieved? Aren't they confirming they're hypocrites? Wouldn't it be consistent with their own rhetoric to say their "silence is violence to Blacks?"*

- *Aren't all institutions who will not speak up about the racism and atrocities of Darwin, Marx, and Sanger, complicit with them and their ongoing cultural legacy? Since all it takes is public denouncement and renouncement of these nefarious miscreants, can't we justifiably say all institutions who don't speak up are anti-Black? Isn't their silence (literally) violence to Blacks (especially due to disproportional effects of eugenics/Black genocide of Planned Parenthood)?*

- *If Darwin and Marx were abjectly evil, aren't those who fully embrace their ideologies and deeds (by definition) evil? Doesn't that mean that clergy embracing Marxist themes are evil, not holy? Aren't schools/education that embrace them also evil? Aren't institutions that embrace them (Darwinism/Marxism) unethical, lacking integry, and evil? If political parties or individuals support socialism/Marxism (including Progressives), then they are (by literal definition and unequivocally) racist and totalitarian (just as Marx dreamed), right?*

CALL TO ACTION!

We've awakened...the "giant" of culture has been "slain" by truth. We uncovered the roots of current racism in America. We've exposed the roots of White Supremacy and now have the ability to chop down the "evil tree" producing bad "fruit." Individuals should no longer have to tolerate and cower under (or make any attempt to appease) the sophomoric drivel of wokesters. When armed with the truth, we have the upper hand.

This book began with the question: "If there is a way to see the entire paradigm of 'race' from its' root,' would you assuredly take a (metaphorical) 'ax' to it to destroy its corrosive impact and effects permanently?" Well? You've read the factually unequivocal evidence, so now what will you do?

After being exposed to historical facts and truth, you should be committed to doing all you can to expose and prevent racism and White Supremacy. The world awaits you...

As a postscript, here is a poignant reminder from theologian C.S Lewis about moving forward with the knowledge conveyed in this book: **"One of the most cowardly things ordinary people do is shut their eyes to facts"** *~ C.S. Lewis*

Now, is the time to redouble efforts to get others WOKE'd Up!

Acknowledgments

This book would not have been possible without great help from my friend and collaborator, Mr. Richard W. Stevens. Mr. Stevens is a brilliant mind. He has depth in understanding today's complex issues, and his editorial prowess helped me tremendously in the refinement of concepts and ideas in this book. Mr. Stevens' work provided impetus and clarity for the completion of this project.

While writing this book, my thought process was heavily influenced by the incredible research and works of Author and Historian William Federer. I used Mr. Federer's research from his American Minute (a free newsletter with remarkable American/world history) throughout. Additionally, I need to acknowledge Dr. Richard Weikart, professor of history at California State University, Stanislaus. This book would have been incomplete without Dr. Weikart's well-documented research on Charles Darwin. His latest book, "Darwinian Racism" is an excellent resource for additional research on Darwin's impact on Hitler, Nazism, and White Nationalism. Lastly, I want to acknowledge the Author and professor of political science at Grove City College. Professor Kengor's groundbreaking exposition on the history of Karl Marx is unparalleled. I highly recommend everyone read his latest book, "The Devil and Karl Marx: Communism's Long March of Death, Deception, and Infiltration."

I acknowledge and personally extend my sincerest thanks to each of the aforementioned scholarly authors and researchers. Your myriad works are warranted and greatly appreciated!

Mr. Terry Barnes must be acknowledged for his impeccable work on the cover design. Terry is an incredible Social Media/Graphic designer with the talent and skills to take meager ideas and turn them into masterpieces; I am incredibly thankful for his work and friendship!

Last but certainly not least, I want to acknowledge the Every Black Life Matters team. This book and associated outcomes (i.e., new paradigms and distinctions, training, etc.) are only possible because you collaborated with helping me to think through and refine ideas carefully. Indeed, Neil's initial guidance and research on Johann Friedrich Blumenbach were critical to this writing. Regina's help with idea refinement, art and animations, and overall Marketing was essential. Lonnie's strong commitment and push to make sure this book comes to fruition were also quite beneficial. The entire EBLM team deserves credit for this book and any good outcomes that may result from it.

A sincere acknowledgment and thanks to all!

Serving you,

Kevin

ENDNOTES

1   Rom. 11:4-5 describes the concept of the "remnant," the people who keep the faith and transmit the truth underground and despite persecution.

2   Victor Davis Hansen, American Greatness, January 24, 2022, https://victorhanson.com/wokeism-is-a-cruel-and-dangerous-cult/

3   "Who Let the Dogs Out," Baha Men, 2010.

4   There is an important difference between "Aryan" and "white." Dr. Richard Weikart, prolific author of books examining the Darwinism-Nazism linkage, stated succinctly in a 2022 interview: "Hitler saw this life as a struggle for existence among many races opposing his so-called Aryan (or sometimes he'd use the term Nordic) race, and he framed it as a Darwinian struggle for existence." The term "Aryan" did not refer to white skin color only, but to a theory that "Aryans" were an ancient superior people that happened to live primarily in northern Europe. Current White Supremacists do conflate the concept of "white" and "Aryan" so that the terms are almost interchangeable when discussing specifically white racism.

5   *The Anthropological Treatises of Johann Friedrich Blumenbach* (1864), available at https://archive.org/details/anthropologicalt00blumuoft

6   Michael Flannery, "Darwin and Race: Three Strikes, He's Out" (Feb. 10, 2021), Evolution News, https://evolutionnews.org/2021/02/darwin-and-race-three-strikes-hes- out/

7   Jerry Bergman, *The Darwin Effect: Its Influence on Nazism, Eugenics, Racism, Communism, Capitalism & Sexism* (New Leaf Pub. Group, 2014).

8   Hear an in-depth interview of Richard Weikart at "Richard Weikart and Hank Hanegraaff Talk Darwinian Racism," ID The Future podcast (Jun. 20, 2022), https://idthefuture.com/1614/

9   Richard Weikart, *Progress through Racial Extermination: Social Darwinism, Eugenics, and Pacifism in Germany, 1860-1918*, German Studies Review 26 (2003), https://doi.org/10.2307/1433326. Prof. Weikart's CV and list of publications available at https://www.csustan.edu/history/Weikart

10   Steven Rowitt, "Darwin's Theory is Racist," https://creationstudies.org/articles/races/390-darwins-theory-racist

11   Bill Federer, "Darwin and Lincoln: Born Exact Same Day – But Lives Had Opposite Effects," (Feb. 11, 2022), https://selfeducatedamerican.com/2019/02/18/charles-darwin-and-abraham-lincoln-born-same-day-lives-have-opposite-impact/

12   "University: Charles Darwin a 'racist' because theory of evolution 'justifies white male superiority'," The College Fix (May 9, 2021),www.thecollegefix.com/university- charles-darwin-a-racist-b-c-theory-of-evolution-justifies-white-male-superiority/, source: Ewan Somerville, "Charles

Darwin's theory of natural selection 'justified white male superiority'," *The Telegraph* (London) (May 8, 2021).

[13] Jules Evans, "Francis Galton and the new religion of Eugenics" (Dec. 3, 2021), (https://www.philosophyforlife.org/blog/pa90euradpo3rpwrn8wpi2jwabluw9)

[14] Francis, Galton, *The History of Twins, As a Criterion of the Relative Powers of Nature and Nurture*, 12 Fraser's Magazine 566 (1875), http://galton.org/essays/1870-1879/galton-1875-history-twins.pdf (accessed Sep. 1, 2017).

[15] Francis Galton, letter to the Editor of *The Times* (Jun. 5, 1873), www.scribd.com/document/155648216/Francis-Galton-Letter-to-Times-1873

[16] Richard Weikart, "Darwinism in Nazi Propaganda," Evolution News (Feb. 23, 2022), https://evolutionnews.org/2022/02/darwinism-in-nazi-propaganda/

[17] Source from Mein Kampf to confirm the attitudes involved: https://www.csustan.edu/history/mein-kampf?msclkid=df6b6a4fc0461 1ec8b7bd29f92db6c54

[18] *Holocaust Encyclopedia*, https://encyclopedia.ushmm.org/index.php/content/en/article/josef-mengele

[19] Marvin Olasky, "Interview: Richard Weikart on how Hitler was Darwin's ideological grandson" (upd. Jun. 28, 2022),www.csustan.edu/history/roots-genocide

[20] Bill Federer, *"Born on the same day, Darwin and Lincoln had opposite views of man,"* World Tribune (Feb. 12, 2018), https://worldtribune.com/life/born-on-the-same-day- darwin-and-lincoln-had-opposite-views-of-man/

[21] Valerie Strauss and Daniel Southerly, "How many died? New evidence suggests far higher numbers for the victims of Mao Zedong's era," Wash. Post (July 17, 1994), https://www.washingtonpost.com/steps-for-disabling-adblocker/2016/09/14/a8c3d4d2-7aac-11e6-bd86-b7bbd53d2b5d_story.html

[22] Michael Flannery, "Paul Johnson's Darwin: A Review," Evolution News (Oct. 23, 2012), https://evolutionnews.org/2012/10/paul_johnsons_d/

[23] https://www.lifesitenews.com/opinion/1-72-billion-abortions-worldwide-in-the-last-40-years/

[24] Margaret Sanger, *Pivot of Civilization* 187 (1922), available at https://archive.org/details/pivotofcivilizat00sanguoft/mode/2up

[25] Margaret Sanger, *Women and the New Race* 63 (New York: Brentano's Publ.,1920), available at https://archive.org/details/in.ernet.dli.2015.150650

[26] *Birth Control Review*, Nov. 1921 (p. 2) (masthead). (Full-text scanned copies of *Birth Control Review* are available at: https://lifedynamics.com/library/#birthcontrol).

[27] Margaret Sanger, "Morality and Birth Control" (Feb. 1918), https://sanger.hosting.nyu.edu/documents/speech_morality_and_bc/

28 "Intelligent or Unintelligent Birth Control?", *Birth Control Review* (May 1919), p. 12.

29 Margaret Sanger, *What Every Girl Should Know* 49 (1913), available in scanned full text at https://lifedynamics.com/library/#birthcontrol

30 Margaret Sanger, *Pivot of Civilization* (1922), and other publications referring to immigrants and poor people" ... 'human weeds,' 'reckless breeders,' 'spawning... human beings who never should have been born." See quotations and citations to sources at Wikiquotes for Margaret Sanger, https://en.wikiquote.org/wiki/Margaret_Sanger. "We do not want word to go out that we want to exterminate the Negro population," Sanger wrote, "if it ever occurs to any of their more rebellious members." (Personal letter dated Dec. 10, 1939, quoted in Linda Gordon, *Woman's Body, Woman's Right: A Social History of Birth Control in America* (1976), also available at https://libex.smith.edu/omeka/files/original/d6358bc3053c93183295bf2df1c0c931.pdf

31 Patrina Mosley, "Margaret Sanger: 'We Want to Exterminate the Negro Population.' Her Wish is Coming True," Lifenews.com (Mar. 10, 2020), www.lifenews.com/2020/03/10/margaret-sanger-we-want-to-exterminate-the-negro- population-her-wish-is-coming-true-2/

32 Becky Yeh, "Planned Parenthood has committed over 7 million abortions since 1970," LifeSite News (Aug. 13, 2015), www.lifesitenews.com/opinion/planned-parenthood-has-committed-over-7-million-abortions-since-1970/

33 Carole Novielli, "Abortions reach highest percentage among Black women since 2000," Live Action News, (Dec. 11, 2019), www.liveaction.org/news/abortions-highest-percentage-black-women-2000/

34 *Box v. Planned Parenthood of Indiana and Kentucky, Inc.*, 587 U.S., 139 S. Ct. 1780 (2019).

35 Paul Johnson, *Intellectuals* (1988).

36 Paul Kengor, *The Devil and Karl Marx: Communism's Long March of Death, Deception, and Infiltration* (2020).

37 Marx to Ferdinand Lassalle in 1861, available at www.marxists.org/archive/marx/works/1861/letters/61_01_16-abs.htm

38 Walter E. Williams, "The Ugly Racism of Karl Marx," Daily Signal, www.dailysignal.com/2017/05/10/ugly-racism-karl-marx/; Walter E. Williams, "Marx, Others Offered Racism," Fairmont Sentinel (Aug. 13, 2020), https://www.fairmontsentinel.com/uncategorized/2020/08/13/marx-others-offered-racism/ ; "Karl Marx and Friedrich Engels Were Not Too Fond of 'Niggers' – So Why Is BLM Run by Marxists?" (Aug. 27, 2020), www.renegadetribune.com/karl-marx-and- friedrich-engels-were-not-too-fond-of-niggers-so-why-is-blm-run-by-marxists/)

39 "Marx and Engels's theory of history: making sense of the race factor." Erik Van Ree, Dec 04, 2018, https://www.tandfonline.com/doi/full/10.1080/13569317.2019.1548094

40 Paul Kengor, The Devil and Karl Marx: Communism's Long March of Death, Deception, and Infiltration (Aug 2020)

41 Paul Johnson, "Marxism vs. the Jews," Commentary (Apr. 1984), www.commentary.org/articles/paul-johnson-3/marxism-vs-the-jews/

42 Richard Dawkins, *The Blind Watchmaker* 6 (London: Penguin Books, 1991 [1986]).

43 Paul Kengor, *The Devil and Karl Marx: Communism's Long March of Death, Deception, and Infiltration* 111-112 (2020).

44 Paul Kengor, *The Devil and Karl Marx: Communism's Long March of Death, Deception, and Infiltration* 30 (2020).

45 Paul Johnson, "Marxism vs. the Jews," Commentary (Apr. 1984), www.commentary.org/articles/paul-johnson-3/marxism-vs-the-jews/

46 Paul Kengor, *The Devil and Karl Marx: Communism's Long March of Death, Deception, and Infiltration* 130 (2020).

47 Paul Kengor, *The Devil and Karl Marx: Communism's Long March of Death, Deception, and Infiltration* 166 (2020).

48 Please see movie "Enemies Within the Church" (2021), https://enemieswithinthechurch.com/ ; Master Notes & Quotes at https://content.enemieswithinthechurch.com/wokepedia_article/master-notes-bibliography/

49 Michael Flannery, "Charles Darwin: Racist Spokesman for Anglo-Male Superiority?", Evolution News (Jul. 14, 2021), https://evolutionnews.org/2021/07/charles-darwin-racist- spokesman-for-anglo-male-superiority-2/

50 Washington Examiner, Matt Peterson, Feb 06, 2012 "Study Saul Alinsky to understand Barack Obama."

51 Washington Examiner, Roger Kimball, Sept 18, 2016 "Want to understand Hillary Clinton? Read Saul Alinsky"

52 Saul Alinsky, Rules For Radicals: A Practical Primer For Realistic Radicals (New York: Random House 1971)- Dedication page

53 David Kupelian, How Evil Works- 1st Threshold Editions hardcover Pg. 240

ADDITIONAL RESOURCES

Every Black Life Matters www.EveryBLM.com :Follow us on all Social Media platforms (YouTube /FB /Instagram /Twitter).

EBLM RaZist ™ **Error! Hyperlink reference not valid.**: For additional information on confronting & combatting racists i.e. Razist training and consulting and/or Hell Razer Advocate certification.

WOKEd UP! www.YallWokedUp.com : For information about the book /book tours and speaking engagements.

Ya'll Woked Up University www.YWUuniversity.com: YouTube & Podcast- Check your favorite podcast providers

Other McGary books via www.Amazon.com :

- "The War On Women from The Root to The Fruit…which side are you on?"

- "Just Justly Justice!"

- "Instanity!"